AF553086

Packaging Techniques

NIPA® GENX ELECTRONIC RESOURCES & SOLUTIONS P. LTD.
New Delhi-110 034

About the Authors

Dr. Tanweer Alam is presently working as an Additional Director & Regional Officer - Indian Institute of Packaging (IIP), Delhi, an autonomous Institute under Ministry of Commerce and Industry, Govt. of India. He is a member of Scientific Committee of Sustainable Packaging, FSSAI. He is also chairman & member of various Technical and Sectional Committees of BIS, CHD 16, CHD 15 & FAD 6. He was Rapporteur in FSSAI - Packaging Regulations. Dr. Alam is an Editior - in - Chief of Journal of Packaging Technology and Research (Springer Publication) and Associate Editor of Journal of Postharvest Technology and Asian Journal of Dairy and Food Research. He is also Editor of Packaging India, a Bimonthly Institutional Magazine and is in Editorial Board of Processed Food Industry. He has guided 5 Ph.D and a dozen of Post Graduate Students. He has been a Mentor for INSA & ICAR Fellows as well. Dr. Alam has published more than 100 research and technical papers in high impact referred journals, apart from delivering several invited lectures both in India and abroad. Spearhead for receiving 21 design patent, 1 granted Indian Patent and filed 3 Indian Patents.

So far, he has published five books on Packaging and Edited dozens of Proceedings, Annual Reports, Vision Documents and Technical Souvenir. He was also the board member of World Packaging Organization (WPO) and Asia Packaging Federation (APF) and has worked as guest faculty at University of Copenhagen, Denmark under faculty exchange programme funded by European Union (EU). Dr. Alam has been a National Fellow of NADSI. He has been a jury member for Asia Star Award. Dr. Alam has organized more than 50 conferences / workshops of National / International stature (Asia Packaging Congress & Research Conclave, ISPI etc.) for promoting packaging and has received several awards and appreciations amongst which Exhibition and Business Excellence Award 2023 given by MSME Global Conference in the recent one. He is spearhead in taking initiative for commencing Six Months Online Certificate Programme on “Packaging & Processing of Fragrance, Flavour & Cosmetics. Dr. Alam is representing as a governing board member FFDC, Kannauj apart from APEDA & GS1. He is also the COURT member of prestigious Guru Gobind Singh Indraprastha University (GGSIPU). He has introduced BS and MS course in Packaging Technology and CPE course in IIP.

Dr. Meenakshi Garg brings a wealth of experience and expertise to her role as Professor at Bhaskaracharya College of Applied Sciences, University of Delhi. With nearly two decades of dedication to teaching Food Science and Technology, Dr. Garg earned her M.Sc. and Ph.D. degrees in Foods and Nutrition from Chaudhary Charan Singh Haryana Agriculture University, Hisar, supplemented by a PG Diploma in Packaging from IIP, Mumbai. Dr. Garg's work has graced over 40 international and national peer-reviewed journals, alongside numerous book chapters and books with esteemed national and international publishers. Her innovative spirit shines through in the form of two awarded patents.

Dr. Garg is not only a prolific researcher but also a sought-after presenter, having delivered numerous oral and poster papers at prestigious national and international conferences. As principal investigator, she has successfully led four major and minor research projects, further solidifying her reputation as a leading expert in food processing and packaging.

Dr Susmita Dey Sadhu is working as a Professor at Department of Polymer Science, at Bhaskaracharya College of Applied Sciences, University of Delhi since 2005. She has completed her Masters in Chemistry (University of Burdwan, WB) followed Ph.D in Rubber Technology from IIT-Kharagpur in 2005. Her research interest includes fields like Packaging, Blend and composites, Nanocomposites and Adhesive applications. She has nearly 450 publications in reputed international journal, 2 patents, nearly 10 book chapters and 3 books published to her credit. She has completed about 5 projects funded by various agencies.

Dr. Prem Lata Meena is working as an Assistant Professor in the Department of Chemistry, Shyam Lal College, University of Delhi. She obtained her Ph.D. in Chemistry from University of Delhi. Dr. Meena has more than 10 years of teaching experience. Her area of research interest Inorganic Polymer Synthesis, Packaging Technology, Food Packaging and Nanotechnology. She also organised and coordinated several Seminars, webinars and Industrial visits. Dr. Meena also served duties as an Observer in many educational bodies and reviewed many National and International journals. Dr. Meena has published several research papers, Books and book chapters in National and International journals. She has also been Awarded in the (Inncvation Project) at University of Delhi and also received best paper awards in various International Conferences.

Packaging Techniques

The Protocol Series Volume 06

Tanweer Alam
Additional Director & Regional Officer
Indian Institute of Packaging (IIP)
Delhi-110092

Meenakshi Garg
Professor
Department of Polymer Science
Bhaskaracharya College of Applied Sciences
Dwarka, New Delhi-110075

Susmita Dey Sadhu
Professor
Department of Polymer Science
Bhaskaracharya College of Applied Sciences
Dwarka, New Delhi-110075

Prem Lata Meena
Assistant Professor
Department of Chemistry
Shyam Lal College
Dwarkapuri, Shahdara, Delhi, 110032

NIPA® GENX ELECTRONIC RESOURCES & SOLUTIONS P. LTD.
New Delhi-110 034

NIPA® GENX ELECTRONIC RESOURCES & SOLUTIONS P. LTD.

101,103, Vikas Surya Plaza, CU Block
L.S.C. Market, Pitam Pura, New Delhi-110 034
Ph : +91-11-43860225, Mob.: +91 9717133558, 9540816132
E-mail: newindiapublishingagency@gmail.com
Website: www.nipaersources.com

© 2025, Publisher

Print ISBN: 978-93-5887-400-6
ebook ISBN: 978-93-5887-439-6

All rights reserved. No part of this publication may be reproduced, stored in a retrieval system or transmitted in any form or by any means, including electronic, mechanical, photocopying recording or otherwise without the prior written permission of the publisher or the copyright holder.

This book contains information obtained from authentic and highly reliable sources. Reasonable efforts have been made to publish reliable data and information, but the author/s, editor/s and publisher cannot assume responsibility for the validity, accuracy or completeness of all materials or information published herein or the consequences of their use. The work is published with the understanding that the publisher and author/s are not attempting to render any professional services. The author/s, editor/s and publisher have attempted to trace and acknowledge the copyright holders of all material reproduced in this publication and apologize to copyright holders if permission and/or acknowledgements to publish in this form have not been taken. If any copyrighted material has not been acknowledged, please write to us and let us know so that we may rectify the error, in subsequent reprints.

Trademark Notice: NIPA®, the NIPA® logos and their presentations (the way they are written/presented) in this book are the trademarks of the publisher and hence may not be used without written permission, if copied or used without authorization, the infringer will be prosecuted as per law.

NIPA® also publishes books in a variety of electronic formats. Some content that appears in print may not be available in electronic books, and vice versa.

Composed and Designed by NIPA®.

Preface

Food packaging is an integral component of the food industry, serving to protect, preserve, and present products in a way that ensures quality and safety from production through consumption. This handbook, designed specifically for students and professionals in food technology and packaging science, provides a comprehensive and practical approach to understanding and conducting essential experiments in food packaging.

This collection of experiments aims to bridge theoretical concepts with hands-on experience, allowing learners to explore various aspects of packaging materials, techniques, and properties. From evaluating packaging material strength and permeability to understanding shelf-life and safety protocols, each experiment in this handbook has been meticulously selected and crafted to foster a solid foundation in food packaging principles.

Structured to encourage critical thinking and skill development, this handbook guides users through each step of the experimental process, offering insights into best practices, potential challenges, and industry-relevant applications. We hope that this resource serves as a valuable tool in preparing future professionals to meet the evolving demands of the food packaging sector with confidence and expertise.

Tanweer Alam
Meenakshi Garg
Susmita Dey Sadhu
Premlata Meena

Contents

Preface ... *vii*

Introduction to Packaging ... 1

1. To Estimate the Sampling Methods and Procedures of Packaging Material ... 13
2. Determination of Water Vapour Transmission Rate of Packaging Material ... 17
3. To Carry Out Sorting of Given Samples by Sink-floatation Technique ... 21
4. To Carry Out Sorting of Given Samples by Selective Dissolution Technique ... 25
5. To Determine the Peel Strength of a Given Samples ... 29
6. To Analyze the Stress-strain Curve of the Polymeric Film (Polystyrene) and Analyse the Curve ... 35
7. To Determine the Tensile Properties of Polymeric Sample ... 39
8. To Determine the Tear Resistance of Polymeric Film ... 43
9. To Determine the Impact Properties of Polymeric Film ... 47
10. To Analyze the Compatibility of Food Packaging Materials Using Shelf-life Studies ... 51
11. To Determine the Caliper/GSM of Paperboard ... 55
12. To Calculate the Burst Strength of the Given Paper and Board ... 57
13. Determination of Water Absorption of Packaging Material by COBB Method ... 59
14. To Calculate the Scuff Resistance of the Printed Sample ... 63

15. To Perform Gas/ Vacuum Packaging of Foods and Study their Shelf Life Studies....65

16. Special Quality Assurance Needs, Good Manufacturing Practices, HACCP, Validation Protocols, etc 69

17. Examination of Canned Food by Cut Out Method 75

18. To Study the Effect of can Close Temperature on the Resultant Vacuum Produced 79

19. To Determine Thermal Shock Resistance in Glass....83

20. Determination of Porosity of Tin Plate 87

21. Identification of Paper and Paperboard....89

22. Edible Packaging of Food Sample 95

23. To Study Physical Tests of Given Sample....97
    I. Determination of Machine Direction....97
    II. Determination of Top Side and Wire Side 97
    III. Determination of Basic Weight or Grammage....98

24. To Study Moisture Content of Given Sample....99

25. To Study Mildew (Fungus) Resistance of Paper & Paper Board Sample....101

26. To Study pH of Given Sample 105

27. To Study Grease Resistance of Given Sample....107

Introduction to Packaging

In today's fast-paced society, packaging is ubiquitous and plays a vital role in the delivery of goods. It serves multiple functions, including containing, protecting, and preserving products from the initial stages of processing and manufacturing to the final point of consumption. Packaging is crucial for efficient handling, transportation, and marketing of goods, particularly in the food industry, where it helps ensure safety, hygiene, and quality. Without effective packaging, the distribution and handling of materials and food items would be cumbersome, inefficient, and prone to significant losses.

The packaging sector represents approximately 2% of the Gross National Product (GNP) in developed countries, with food packaging alone accounting for nearly half of this figure. According to Lockhart (1997), packaging is defined as a socio-scientific discipline that functions within society to ensure that goods reach the ultimate consumer in the intended condition.

Understanding the distinction between the terms "package," "packing," and "packaging" is crucial. A "package" is the physical entity that encloses or contains a product. While "packing" and "packaging" are often mistakenly considered synonymous, they represent different stages in the process of preparing goods for distribution. "Packing" involves preparing a product for transportation and storage, focusing primarily on protection during transit. On the other hand, "packaging" encompasses preparing a product not only for storage and transport but also for sale, playing a critical role in marketing and promotion. Thus, while packing focuses on logistics, packaging extends to include consumer engagement and brand communication.

Effective packaging is essential for every type of food product, whether fresh or processed. It acts as a critical link between the producer and the consumer, and a lack of attention to packaging can result in product spoilage, damage, and customer dissatisfaction. The technological and design investments in food products are rendered ineffective if the packaging does not ensure their delivery in optimal condition.

Societal Benefits of Packaging

Prevention of Food Spoilage and Product Damage: Packaging helps in preserving the nutritional attributes and quality of food products by protecting them from external environmental factors.

- Cost Efficiency: By enabling mass production and bulk distribution, packaging reduces the cost of food and other commodities.
- Reduction of Adulteration and Tampering: Packaging acts as a barrier against tampering, ensuring that products remain uncontaminated and safe for consumption.
- Hygienic and Attractive Presentation: It ensures that food products are presented in a manner that is both hygienic and visually appealing to consumers.
- Facilitates Informed Purchase: Packaging provides vital information such as ingredients, nutritional facts, expiration dates, and storage instructions, aiding consumers in making informed decisions.
- Enhanced Consumer Choice: A variety of packaging options allows consumers to select products based on their preferences, such as portion size, material type, and convenience.
- Energy Conservation: Efficient packaging methods like ambient packs help in energy conservation during storage and transport.
- Year-Round Availability: Packaging ensures that food products are available throughout the year, regardless of seasonal variations or geographic limitations.

Functions of Packaging

Packaging serves several essential functions that contribute to its effectiveness and importance:

- Containment: Packaging holds the product securely, ensuring that it can be transported and stored without leakage or damage. Proper containment minimizes product loss and environmental pollution. A robust seal prevents leakage and protects both the product and the environment.
- Protection: The primary role of packaging is to protect its contents from external influences, such as physical damage, chemical contamination, or microbiological spoilage. Effective packaging extends the shelf life of food products by acting as a barrier against spoilage agents, including oxygen, moisture, and microorganisms.
- Convenience: Modern consumers prefer packaging that is easy to handle store, and use. For example, flexible retort pouches for condiments

which are easier to store and use compared to traditional glass bottles demonstrate convenience in packaging. Packages that are resealable easy to open, or designed for single-use enhance consumer satisfaction and can boost sales.

- Communication: Packaging serves as a silent salesman, conveying critical information about the product to consumers. It provides essential details such as nutritional content, product origin, usage instructions, and regulatory compliance marks (e.g., vegetarian and non-vegetarian symbols). Effective communication through packaging builds consumer trust and facilitates informed purchasing decisions.

Classification of Packaging

Packaging can be categorized based on various factors such as shape, levels contents, method, and material:

Based on Shape (Form and Size)

- Heavy Packaging: Designed to withstand the physical demands of transportation, includes large containers and wooden boxes.
- Medium Packaging: Smaller than heavy packaging, typically includes carton boxes, cans, and barrels.
- Light Packaging: Includes small, flexible packages like pouches, bottles and paper containers, which are easy to transport and handle.

Based on Levels

- Primary Packaging: The first layer that directly contacts the product such as glass containers or plastic wraps.
- Secondary Packaging: Protects both the product and its primary packaging, often used for display purposes, such as cardboard boxes.
- Tertiary Packaging: Used for bulk handling, storage, and transport typically not visible to the consumer (e.g., pallets, shrink wrap).

Based on Contents

- Packaging varies depending on the type of product, such as food cosmetics, pharmaceuticals, clothing, and hazardous materials.

Based on Method

- Vacuum Packaging: Involves removing air from the package to prevent oxidation and extend shelf life.
- Aseptic Packaging: Sterile packaging used for products like milk and juices to maintain sterility over time.

- Modified Atmosphere Packaging (MAP): Uses a mix of gases to extend shelf life and preserve quality.
- Skin Packaging: Involves wrapping the product in a plastic film that conforms to its shape and seals it onto a paperboard.

Based on Material

- Rigid Packaging: Made from materials like glass and metal, providing structural support and protection.
- Semi-Rigid Packaging: Offers moderate flexibility and protection typically made from materials like plastic containers.
- Flexible Packaging: Made from materials like films and foils, providing high adaptability and easy handling.

Materials Used in Food Packaging

Packaging design and construction are crucial to the shelf life of a food product. Choosing the appropriate packaging materials and technologies is essential to maintain product quality and freshness during transportation and storage. Traditionally, materials such as glass, metals (including aluminum foils, laminates, tinplate, and tin-free steel), paper, paperboard, and various plastics have been used for food packaging.

1. Glass

Glass has a long history as a food packaging material. It is produced by heating a mixture of silica (the glass former), sodium carbonate (the melting agent), and limestone or calcium carbonate along with aluminum (stabilizers) to high temperatures. This mixture melts into a thick liquid mass that is then shaped into containers through molding. Glass containers often undergo surface coating to provide lubrication during production, reduce scratching or surface abrasion, and prevent line jams. These coatings also enhance and preserve the strength of the glass, reducing the risk of breakage.

Advantages of Glass

Odorless and Chemically Inert: Glass does not react with most food products maintaining their flavor and quality.

Impermeability: Glass is impermeable to gases and vapors, preserving product freshness and flavor for extended periods.

Heat Resistance: Glass can withstand high processing temperatures, making it ideal for the heat sterilization of both low and high-acid foods.

Rigidity and Insulation: Glass offers good rigidity and thermal insulation and can be molded into various shapes and sizes.

Transparency: Glass allows consumers to see the product, while variations in color can protect light-sensitive contents.

Environmental Benefits: Glass is reusable and recyclable, contributing to environmental sustainability.

Disadvantages of Glass

Weight: Glass is heavy, which increases transportation costs.

Fragility: It is brittle and susceptible to breakage due to internal pressure, impact, or thermal shock.

2. Metals

Metals are among the most versatile packaging materials, offering excellent physical protection, barrier properties, formability, decorative potential recyclability, and consumer acceptance. The primary metals used in packaging include aluminum and steel.

Aluminum

Applications: Used in making cans, foils, and laminated paper or plastic packaging.

Properties: Light in weight, derived from bauxite ore, with magnesium and manganese added to improve strength. It has excellent corrosion resistance due to a natural coating of aluminum oxide, which offers a barrier against air temperature, moisture, and chemicals.

Flexibility and Recyclability: Aluminum is flexible, malleable, and ideal for recycling as it can be easily processed into new products.

Usage: Pure aluminum is often used in lightweight packaging, such as soft drink cans, pet food containers, and seafood packaging.

Aluminum Foil

Manufacturing: Created by rolling pure aluminum into thin sheets and then annealing to achieve dead-folding properties, allowing it to be folded tightly.

Barrier Properties: Provides excellent resistance to moisture, air, odors, light, and microorganisms. It is inert to acidic foods and generally does not require additional protection such as lacquer.

Laminates and Metallized Films

Laminates: Involve bonding aluminum foil to paper or plastic film to enhance barrier properties. Laminated packaging is often used for high-value food products like dried soups, herbs, and spices, but it is relatively expensive.

Metallized Films: A more cost-effective alternative to laminated packaging. These are plastics with a thin layer of aluminum metal, offering improved barrier properties against moisture, oils, air, and odors.

Tinplate

Description: Produced from low-carbon steel, coated with a thin layer of tin on both sides.

Properties: Provides good barrier properties against gases, water vapor, light, and odors. Tinplate containers can be heat treated and hermetically sealed, making them suitable for sterile products.

Applications: Used for cans, containers for powdered foods, confections, and packaging closures.

Advantages: Lightweight, strong, ductile, and less expensive than aluminum. It is also compatible with modern coating and printing technologies, allowing for decorative packaging.

Tin-Free Steel (TFS)

Description: Also known as electrolytic chromium or chrome oxide-coated steel, TFS requires an organic coating to provide corrosion resistance.

Properties: Has good adhesion for coatings like paints, lacquers, and inks, along with excellent formability and strength.

Applications: Commonly used for food cans, bottle caps, closures, and trays.

3. Plastics

Plastics are synthetic materials made through two main types of polymerization: condensation polymerization (polycondensation) and addition polymerization (polyaddition).

Polycondensation: Involves reactions between molecules that release by-products like water or methanol. It requires monomers with at least two functional groups (alcohol, amine, carboxylic).

Polyaddition: Involves combining two or more molecules without producing by-products, forming larger polymer chains.

Plastics offer significant design flexibility, being moldable into various shapes and sizes. They are lightweight, chemically inert, and available in a wide range of physical and optical properties. Plastics are also heat-sealable, easy to print on, and integrate well into production processes where packaging is formed, filled, and sealed in a single line.

Disadvantages of Plastics

Variable Permeability: Plastics have different degrees of permeability to light, gases, vapors, and low-molecular-weight molecules, which can affect the shelf life of some food products.

The use of plastics in food packaging continues to rise due to their cost-effectiveness and functional advantages, such as thermo-sealability, microwave compatibility, and adaptability to unlimited shapes and sizes.

Types of Plastics Used in Food Packaging

Polyolefins: Include polyethylene (PE) and polypropylene (PP), which are among the most widely used plastics in food packaging.

Polyethylene (PE): Made by the addition polymerization of ethylene. It comes in two primary types:

High-Density Polyethylene (HDPE): Stiff, strong, tough, and resistant to chemicals and moisture. Used for making bottles, grocery bags, and containers.

Low-Density Polyethylene (LDPE): Flexible, strong, and easy to seal, commonly used for bags, lids, and squeeze bottles.

Polypropylene (PP): Harder, denser, and more transparent than PE, with good resistance to chemicals and water vapor. It is suitable for hot-fill and microwaveable applications like yogurt containers.

Polyester: Condensation polymers formed from ester monomers, such as polyethylene terephthalate (PET or PETE).

PET (Polyethylene Terephthalate): Provides a good barrier against gases and moisture. It is resistant to heat, oils, and acids and is widely used for beverage bottles due to its transparency, lightweight, and shatter resistance.

Polyvinyl Chloride (PVC): An addition polymer of vinyl chloride, known for its resistance to chemicals and grease, although it poses challenges in recycling.

4. Paper and Paperboard

Paper and paperboard have been used in food packaging since the 17th century. They are commonly employed in corrugated boxes, milk cartons, folding cartons, bags, sacks, and wrapping paper. Different types of paper packaging materials include:

Paper

Plain paper has poor barrier properties and is not heat-sealable, so it is often treated, coated, laminated, or impregnated with substances like waxes, resins, or lacquers to improve its properties.

Types of Paper

Kraft Paper: Used for small bags or wrappers for biscuits and confectionery.

Sulphite Paper: Used for wrapping snack foods, cookies, candy bars, and other oily foods.

Glassine: Serves as a liner for biscuits, cooking fats, fast foods, and baked goods.

Parchment Paper: Suitable for packaging fats like butter and lard.

Paperboard

Description: Made in multiple layers, resulting in higher weight per unit area. Commonly used for containers like boxes, cartons, and trays.

Types of Paperboard

White Board, Solid Board, Chipboard, Fibreboard: Used for various packaging applications.

Paper Laminates

Laminated paper involves bonding paper with plastic or aluminum to improve properties like heat sealability and barrier quality. Although it enhances packaging performance, it also increases costs. Laminated paper is often used for packaging products like soups, herbs, and spices.

Ancillary material

It is a secondary packaging material that adds value to primary packaging. Its absence or inadequacy can impair the function of the primary package. These materials also add value to the product. The ancillary materials along with the primary materials provide:

- Product – package compatibility,
- It prevents contamination,
- Enhances visibility,
- Holds packaging material,
- Gives strength,
- Protection of products from any damage.

Some of the important ancillary materials include:

- Adhesives,
- Printing inks,
- Labels,

- Caps and closures,
- Reinforcement materials such as tapes and straps.

The packages that come in direct contact with the food material, the safety aspects are applied to both primary and ancillary materials. Examples are adhesives for laminates, printing inks for food packages, caps and closures for bottles and containers.

Adhesives

Adhesive bonding is the process of joining materials with the help of a substance that is capable of holding such materials together by surface attachment. Polymers are widely used as adhesives.

The primary function of adhesive is to unite parts together. Adhesives do this by transmitting stress from one surface to another in a manner that distributes the stress uniformly that can be achieved with conventional mechanical fasteners.

Classification of adhesives

Adhesives are classified as

- Waterborne adhesives
- Hot – melt adhesives
- Solvent – borne adhesives

Waterborne adhesives: this is the oldest and still the largest volume class of adhesive used in packaging. Advantages of using these adhesives are:

- Ease and safety of handling,
- Energy efficiency,
- Low cost,
- High strength

Waterborne adhesives can further be differentiated into two categories: Natural and Synthetic.

- Natural waterborne adhesives include starch, proteins, animal glue, and casein and rubber latex.
- Synthetic waterborne adhesives are most widely used adhesives in packaging. These are resin emulsions, specifically polyvinyl acetate emulsions – stable suspensions of polyvinyl acetate particles in water.

Hot – melt adhesives: hot melts can be defined as 100% solid adhesive based on thermoplastic polymers that are applied when in the molten state and set to hold and form bonds on cooling and solidification. Their biggest advantage is the extremely rapid rate of bond formation, which leads to high production rates on a packaging line.

The most commonly used material as the backbone of hot melts is the co – polymer of Ethylene and Vinyl Acetate. These copolymers have an excellent balance of molten stability, adhesion and toughness over a broad temperature range, as well as compatibility with many modifiers.

Solvent – borne adhesives: these are the class of adhesives rarely used in packaging and find use in specialized applications where waterborne or hot – melt systems do not meet the technical requirements. Rubber resin solutions are still used as pressure – sensitive adhesives for labels and tapes. Factors of cost, safety, productivity and compliance with clean air law are some of the concerns related to the use of solvent – borne adhesives.

Solvented polyurethane adhesives play a vital role in flexible packaging for the lamination of plastic films. These multilayer films find applications in bags, pouches, snack food wrap, meat and cheese packs and boil – in bag food pouches.

Important adhesives and their applications

Adhesives	Applications
Acrylics	Pressure sensitive coating, Heat seal coating
Ethylene- vinyl acetate co – polymer hot melt	High speed packaging operations. Wrap around case sealing.
Polyurethanes	Flexible laminates for food packaging – cover a large spectrum from heat resistant confectionary films to boil – in – bag / oven able laminates
Polyvinyl acetate	Cold set corrugating lap- glue, case sealing, carton sealing, tube winding
Polyvinyl alcohol	Solid board lamination, tube winding
Styrene – butadiene and styrene – isoprene block co – polymers	Label stock, tapes

Laminating adhesives for flexible packaging of processed food

Flexible packaging materials are used extensively for packaging processed food and a wide range of other products. These packaging materials are made from plastic films, aluminium foil and various types of paper. "Dry adhesive lamination" is a process that is very commonly used to produce laminated flexible packaging.

Laminating adhesives are classified according to their functional properties (i.e., bond strength, chemical resistance, heat resistance) as follows:

- General purpose
- Medium performance
- High performance
- Ultra high performance

General purpose adhesives are most economical and are used for low requirement, relatively simple end – uses. General purpose applications include packaging of snack food and non – aggressive dry products. The relatively more expensive medium, high and ultra-high performance adhesives are used in laminates where higher thermal and/ or chemical resistance is required.

Printing inks

Printing inks are colored liquids or pastes, formulated to transfer and reproduce an image from a printing surface. They are used mainly to convey a message and also provide protection and provide a decorative effect. These are used on a wide range of materials like papers, boards, plastic, and glass and textiles.

Inks used for food packages

Food packaging inks are classified into the following:

- Inks for external packaging: this is any packaging additional to an immediate food wrapping and the printed matter has a barrier in the form of another wrapper between it and the food. These materials used for printing inks have to be non – toxic.
- Inks used for immediate food wrapping: when the printed matter is directly in contact with the food material, such as butter wrapper, ice cream wrapper.

It is necessary that inks for this purpose must be on the outside of the wrapper, which itself acts as a barrier. And the reverse printing of the films must be avoided.

It must be taken into consideration that printing inks are not food additives and therefore must not be used in direct contact with the food.

Latest trend

- UV and Water based inks and coatings: radiation curing technology add value to the product due to the following advantages – high gloss finishes, better chemical and solvent resistance, high rub and abrasion resistance, better print resolution, instant drying and low odors.
- Universal ink concept: universal ink concept has been developed for flexible packaging using gravure and flexo processes. Advantages of universal ink systems are:

  i) Very low solvent retention in the print.

  ii) Trouble free running at maximum speed

  iii) Instant adhesion on substrates.

Labels: it can be defined as a slip of paper, card or metal attached to an object that indicates its nature, owner, name and other properties. The process of attaching a label to any object is termed as labelling; it can be done with simple manual operations or through automated technology.

Types of labels

- Non – adhesive label materials
  i) Glue applied: wet glue, hot – melt glue
  ii) Shrink/stretch sleeve: formed into tube and shrunk on with heat, formed into tube and stretched over object
  iii) In mould: placed in mould prior to injection or blow moulding
- Pre – adhesive label materials
  i) Gummed – activate with water
  ii) Heat activated – activate with heat
  iii) Pressure sensitive – protective backing removed then applied with pressure

Shelf life: It is the time period that food products are given before they are considered unsuitable for consumption or sale.. It is the time period between the production and packaging of a food product when it becomes unacceptable under defined environmental conditions. It is a function of the package, product and the environment through which the product is stored, transported and sold.

Experiment 1

To Estimate the Sampling Methods and Procedures of Packaging Material

Objective

After performing this experiment, you will be able to learn

Sampling methods and procedures of packaging material.

Introduction

The objective of sampling of a packaging material is to obtain a representative sample of a whole lot for the required testing and/or grading. It is expected that the test results and grading will reflect the average quality of the PM from which the sample was taken.

Principle

The sample techniques and processes outlined in this publication are grounded upon scientific principles. Since the validity of any later test result depends on the quality of the sampling and the information given with the sample, the sampler is essential to the process of selecting lots for testing and/or grading.

Every PM in the population being sampled has an equal chance of being selected, according to the random sampling principle. Usually, the sample size that is tested is very small in relation to the size of the lot that it represents. The sample must be taken carefully and in a way that gives assurance that it is genuinely representative of the lot. Similarly, in order to reduce the composite sample, all necessary.

Procedure

It is established to provide the guidelines for sampling of packaging material.

1. Affix packaging material identification slip with all necessary information on each container of the same lot together with a quarantine label, data of sampling, name of person and signature.
2. During sampling the quality assurance personnel will give all details of the quarantine label regarding date of sampling name of person and signature

Conditions Before Sampling

a) Packing materials are placed in the Quarantine Area, properly labeled.

b) Condition of the container – it should not be damaged, torn, contaminated with dust, water etc.

c) In case of any abnormalities, all details should be noted on packing material receiving receipt

d) Each uniform looking delivery of packaging materials is considered as one batch

e) Primary packaging materials are to be considered equivalent to raw materials as far as quality is concerned.

Procedure of sampling

1. Record relevant information about packaging material.
2. Take out Photocopy of Sampler's Checklist.
3. The separate sampler's remark shall be used for each lot of Batches.
4. Prepare the "UNDER TEST" label from the computer system to affix on the consignment.
5. Check the delivered items to ensure that the quantity received corresponds with the GRN Quantity.
6. Fill the necessary details in Sampler's Check List by taking the reference of Goods Receipt Note (GRN). If discrepancy found in GRN inform the warehouse for corrective action.
7. Go to the Quarantine area and identify the material to be sampled from the Quarantined label which is affixed by Warehouse on the packs.
8. In case of Aluminium and PVC foils carry out the sampling under Laminar Air Flow (LAF).
9. Cleaning of LAF shall be carried out on every alternate day or early if required. The LAF shall be cleaned with wet mop followed by dry mop.
10. The cleaning shall be recorded in the cleaning record for LAF
11. Ensure that the surrounding area is clean, if not get it clean, prior to the start of the sampling.
12. Check the packing condition of the material and details mentioned on the Under Test labels.
13. Verify that the Quarantine Labels are affixed by Warehouse Personnel.
14. In case of any discrepancies intimate to Executive / Head - Quality Assurance or Head - Quality Control for necessary action.

15. Ensure that packs are cleaned externally and open the packages only after ensuring the proper cleaning. Observe the material for any abnormalities and record it on the Sampler's Checklist.
16. Check the following points during sampling of the material:
    - Mode of packing,
    - Indication of packing,
    - Details available on pack (Containers), No. of packs (containers) received,
    - Total quantity received,
    - No. of packs (containers) sampled,
    - Quantity to be sampled.
    - Name of the person who sampled along with date of sampling.
17. Withdraw the samples randomly by opening different containers / Boxes as per n +1 and take out sampling quantity for visual inspection as per sampling plan MIL – STD 105D Acceptable Quality Level (AQL).
18. Note down the sampled quantity in Sampler's checklist based on the number of packages to be sampled.
19. Examine the sampled material as per AQL against the approved standard for general appearance, deviation from normal visual quality, color, text etc. wherever applicable.
20. Record the results in the approved Visual Inspection Report for Aluminium foil and PVC Foil.
21. After completion of sampling the material pack shall be resealed with BOPP Tape or tied with the help of cable – tie.
22. Affix the "UNDER TEST" to all the rolls of sticker labels, foils and every container of rubber plugs. For all other packaging materials at least one "UNDER TEST" Label shall be affixed on bottom container/ pack of each pallet.
23. Affix the SAMPLED BY QC sticker label duly signed and mentioning the container number according to sampling plan, on the outer container of the material from which sample is taken.
24. Check that the number of packs is correct as mentioned in the test label.
25. Take out a composite sample for analysis as per respective Packing Material Specifications. Put the sampled quantity in self-sealing polybag bearing the label of "SAMPLE FOR ANALYSIS"

26. Carry out testing of the packaging material as per the laid down specifications of respective material.
27. The sampling procedure described above will not be applicable for Tertiary Packaging material like Shipper, pad, partition and corrugated trays. For these materials only one unit shall be collected and carry out the analysis as per laid down specification

1.4 Observation

Packaging material				
Batch no.				
Date of receipt				
Quantity received				

1.5 Inference

The accuracy with which the results of analyses represent the lot depends upon:

a) The homogeneity of the lot from which the sample is drawn;
b) Whether the sampling is done in a manner that ensures that the sample is randomly selected;
c) The use of sampling equipment appropriate to the crop type and the program for which the sampling is taken;
d) The care used in drawing the samples;
e) The care with which the primary samples are mixed to obtain the composite sample;
f) The care used in mixing and dividing the composite sample to obtain the required subsamples for testing; and
g) The integrity of the primary, composite and submitted sample(s) and the information provided with the submitted sample(s).

Experiment 2

Determination of Water Vapour Transmission Rate of Packaging Material

Objective

After performing this experiment, you will be able to learn:

Water vapour transmission rate of packaging material

Introduction

Moisture Vapor Transmission Rate (MVTR), also known as Water Vapor Transmission Rate (WVTR), measures the rate at which water vapor passes through a material. MVTR is crucial in various industries where moisture control is vital. For example, moisture-sensitive foods and pharmaceuticals are packaged using materials with controlled MVTR to ensure quality, safety, and shelf life. In the textile industry, MVTR serves as a measure of breathability, enhancing comfort for outdoor clothing. In the building materials industry, managing moisture barrier properties in architectural components helps maintain appropriate moisture levels in the internal spaces of buildings.

Various techniques are used to measure MVTR, ranging from gravimetric methods that assess moisture gain or loss by mass to advanced instrumental techniques capable of measuring extremely low transmission rates. It's important to note that special care must be taken when measuring porous substances like fabrics, as some techniques may not be suitable.

The conditions under which MVTR measurements are taken-such as temperature and humidity gradients across the sample-greatly influence the results. Therefore, an MVTR result must specify these conditions; otherwise, the data becomes unreliable. Comparisons between two results should only be made when conditions are known. The most common international unit for MVTR is grams per square meter per day ($g/m^2/day$). In the USA, grams per 100 square inches per day ($g/100\ in^2/day$) is also used, which is roughly 1/15 of the value in $g/m^2/day$. Typical MVTR rates can range from as low as 0.001 $g/m^2/day$ for aluminum foil laminates to several thousand $g/m^2/day$ for fabrics.

Factors Affecting WVTR Values

- **Thickness**
- **Resin Composition**
  - Molecular weight distribution
  - Crystallinity/density
  - Chain length and chain length distribution
  - Chain orientation
- **Polymer Blends**
- **Additives**
- **Coatings:** Such as PVdC or metalizing

Application of WVTR in Food Packaging

WVTR is critical in food packaging, where one of the main functions is to maintain the desired moisture level of the product. For instance, packaging keeps dry products like potato chips, pretzels, and fortune cookies dry, while retaining moisture in products like cheese, muffins, and chewing gum. Without adequate moisture barrier protection, these products would quickly reach equilibrium with the environmental relative humidity, leading to undesirable texture changes (e.g., crispy products becoming soggy or chewy products becoming hard and dry). WVTR serves as the standard measure to compare films for their ability to resist moisture transmission. Lower WVTR values indicate better moisture protection, ensuring quality control and improving storage, transportation, and shelf life of food products.

Materials Required

- Open-mouth dish of non-corrodible material
- Anhydrous calcium chloride ($CaCl_2$)
- Microcrystalline wax
- Crystalline wax
- Analytical balance
- Environmental chamber

Procedure

1. Prepare the Dish: Fill an aluminum or glass dish with anhydrous calcium chloride ($CaCl_2$), dried at 200°C, in the form of small lumps (2 to 2.5 mm).
2. Fill with Desiccant: Ensure the desiccant fills the dish up to within 6 mm of the specimen, leaving enough space for easy mixing by shaking.

3. Prepare the Specimen: Cut a specimen with uniform surfaces and fix it to the dish using molten wax. The wax should be a mixture of 60% microcrystalline wax and 40% refined crystalline wax, combined with resins in equal weights.
4. Seal the Specimen: Ensure the sealant is applied correctly to prevent any leakage of water vapor.
5. Weigh the Assembly: Measure the entire assembly on an analytical balance.
6. Place in Environmental Chamber: Position the assembly in an environmental chamber maintained at 37.8°C and 90% relative humidity, ensuring proper air circulation over the assembly.
7. Monitor Weight Changes: Weigh the assembly at regular intervals.
8. Analyze Data: Plot the gain in weight against time to assess moisture vapor transmission.

Observations

Temprature

Relative humidity

Diameter of sample

Radius of sample

Day	Weight(g)

Calculations

$A = \pi\gamma_2$

$= cm^2$

$$WVTR = \frac{g \times 24}{T \times a}$$

g = weight gain or loss

T = time in hrs. during which gain or loss occur

a = exposed area of specimen m^2

Inference

Precautions

Sealing with wax should be done carefully.

Note the weight properly. Shaking should be done at each weighing.

Note the RH and temperature accurately.

Experiment 3

To Carry Out Sorting of Given Samples by Sink-floatation Technique

Objective

After performing this experiment, you will be able to learn

Sorting of samples by sink-floatation technique.

Introduction

Sink float is the simplest and cheapest method among all the wet sorting techniques in which polymers are separated based on their density. This technique is extremely fast, environment friendly and cost effective process for sorting of plastics. Since, the separations are done based on density, so any factor which may change the density of the pure polymer like blending, composite formation of multilayer structures etc. will not be separated well using this method. Moreover, if any two polymers are very close in density, they cannot be separated easily. That is why PVC and PET which are very close in their density can not be separated using sink floatation method.

Initially the plastic waste is added to the container containing water and the system is gently stirred to evenly wet the surface of plastic and remove any air trapped on the surface. Since the density of polyolefins is near/close to each other but lighter than water, they all float in water whereas the heavier plastics sink. This technique is primarily used to separate polyolefins from other plastics. Now to further segregate the polyolefinic fraction, this method is extended by adding the polyolefin mixture to another container containing water and alcohol. As dropwise more and more alcohol are added to the water, the density of the medium will decrease and the polyolefins start separating. For separating the heavier fraction of the polymer, the mixture of polymers is added to water. To this water, dropwise salt water is added and stirred. Salt water increases the density of the medium slowly and at one point, the polymers which were sinking in water, will start floating depending on their density.

S.No.	Polymer	Density (g/cm3)
1	PVC (Polyvinyl Chloride)	1.4
2	PS (Polystyrene)	1.04
3	PET (Polyethylene Terephthalate)	1.38
4	HDPE (High Density Polyethylene)	0.94-0.96
5	LLDPE (Linear Low Density Polyethylene)	0.91-0.94
6	PP (Polypropylene)	0.92

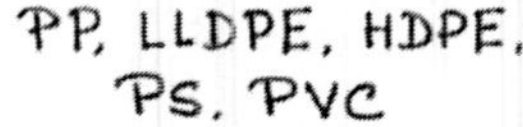

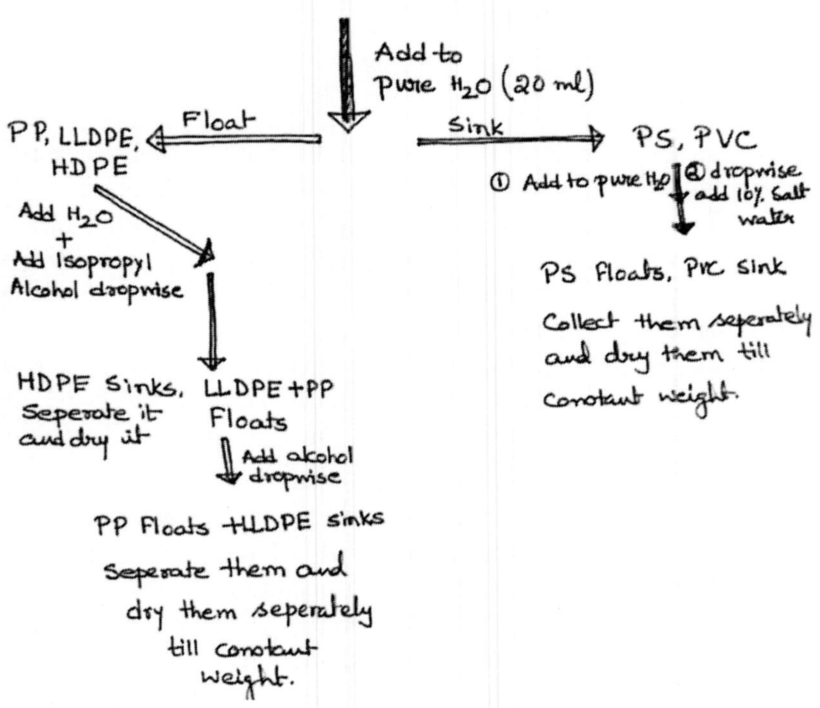

Apparatus: Beaker, measuring cylinder, glass rod, Filter paper

Materials Required: LLDPE, HDPE, PP, PS, PVC, Water, Isopropyl Alcohol, salt

Procedure

- Take 1g of each polymer sample and mix them.
- Add the mixture in beaker containing water with stirring and separate the floating and the sinking samples (HDPE & LLDPE will float and PS & PVC will sink)

HDPE & LLDPE (floated part)

- Take 20 ml of water and add the separated floated samples (HDPE & LLDPE).
- Now start adding alcohol (isopropyl alcohol) dropwise and at one point one of them will sink and one remain floated (HDPE will sink and LLDPE will float).
- Separate the sample and dry them in oven at 50°C
- After drying weigh and record the recovered weight and calculate the percentage of recovery.
- Calculate the density of the solution obtained after mixing water and alcohol

PVC & PS (sinked part)

- Take 20 ml of water and add the separated floated samples (PS & PVC).
- Take 5g of NaCl salt and dissolve it in 50ml of water in a beaker (10% NaCl solution).
- Now start adding Salt solution (NaCl) dropwise and at one point one of them will sink and one will floated (PVC will sink and PS will float).
- Separate the sample and dry them in oven at 50°C.
- After drying weigh and record the recovered weight and calculate the percentage of recovery.
- Calculate the density of the solution obtained after mixing water and NaCl solution.

Observations

For HDPE & LLDPE

Weight of beaker =

Weight of beaker + solution obtain =

Weight of solution obtain =

Volume of solution obtain =

Density = mass / volume =g/cm^3

Percentage of recovery

HDPE

..............................%

LLDPE

...............................%

For PVC & PS

Weight of beaker = ……………..g

Weight of beaker + solution obtain = ……………..g

Weight of solution obtain = ……………..g

Volume of solution obtain = …………….ml

Density = mass / volume = ……………………………g/cm^3

Percentage of recovery

PS

……………………………..%

PVC

………………………………%

Result

- Density of solution formed (alcohol + water) = …………..g/cm^3
- Density of solution formed (salt solution + water) = …………..g/cm^3
- Percentage recovery

  HDPE = ………..%

  LLDPE = ………..%

  PVC = ………..%

  PS = ………..%

Inference

Precautions

1. The granules should be wet properly

Advantages

1. Very simple, fast and environment friendly

Disadvantages

1. Can not separate PVC and PET effectively as the densities of PVC and PET are very close.

Experiment 4

To Carry Out Sorting of Given Samples by Selective Dissolution Technique

Objective

After performing this experiment, you will be able to learn

Sorting of given samples by selective dissolution technique.

Introduction

Sorting process is the process of separating the mingled and mixed plastic before the recycling process.

Selective Dissolution Technique (SDP)

Recycling of plastic has become the major focus nowadays. Sorting of plastic materials is the major step towards recycling. One of the sorting techniques is selective dissolution although it has not found major usage in industry for various drawbacks. This technique uses the solubility parameter of different polymers for segregation purpose. Each polymer owing to its chemical structure has different solubility parameters. Hence, the solvents for each and every polymer are different. This difference in solubility in different solvents is used here for separating them from one another.

There are two types of selective dissolution technique, namely single solvent technique and multiple solvent technique. In single solvent technique one single solvent (generally, Xylene) is used to dissolve different polymers at different conditions. After, dissolving each polymer the xylene solution is taken separately and is flash volatilized at low pressure. This solvent is then again used to dissolve the next polymer in the mixture under different condition. This way step by step, each polymer can be separated and dried.

In the second method namely, multi solvent technique, the polymers are separated using various solvents depending on the solubility parameters. In this case the solubilization and the separation is not done under severe conditions.

Sl No.	Polymer	Common Solvent
1	PVC (Polyvinyl Chloride)	Tetrahydrofuran
2	PS (Polystyrene)	Benzene at Rocm Temperature or toluene
3	PET (Polyethylene Terephthalate)	Ethylene glycol
4	HDPE (High Density Polyethylene)	Trichlorobenzene or cyclohexane
5	LLDPE (Linear Low Density Polyethylene)	Trichlorobenzene or cyclohexane
6	PP (Polypropylene)	TCB + 0.015% BHT
7	PMMA	Benzene at elevated temperature (more than 30°C)
8	Nylon 66	Formic Acid
9	Polyvinyl Alcohol	Hot water

Flow chart

	Mixture of polymers		
Soluble (PS)	BENZENE OR TOLUENE		Insoluble (PVC, PP)
	Tetrahydrofuran		
Insoluble		Soluble	
PP		PVC	
	Mixture of polymers		
Soluble part			Insoluble part
Can be purified by Precipitation, by adding			
Non solvent. The precipitate is then washed is extruded			
	Solvent removal		Sclid polymer

Diagram

Procedure

Apparatus: Beaker, measuring cylinder, magnetic bead

Polymer: PS, PVC, PP

Procedure

- Take 1g of each polymer sample and mix them.
- Take the polymer samples in beaker and add benzene or toluene and stir it at room temperature.
- **PS** will dissolve in benzene or toluene. Filter the SOLUTION and separate remaining solid samples from solution.
- Add alcohol (non-solvent) in solution to precipitate PS.
- Filter the precipitate and dry it in electric oven.
- Weigh and record the weight recovered.
- Take the solid sample left in another beaker and add THF and stir at room temperature.
- PVC will dissolve in THF filter the extract and separate remaining solid PP from solution.
- Add alcohol (non-solvent) in solution to precipitate PVC.
- Filter the precipitate and dry it in electric oven.
- Weigh and record the weight recovered.

- PP will left behind in solid state. Dry it and record weight recovery.

Observation

For PS

Weight recovered = …………g

For PVC

Weight recovered = …………g

For PP

Weight recovered = ………….g

Percentage of recovery

PS ……………………………%

PVC ……………………………%

PP ………………………….....%

Precautions

1. The granules should be dissolved properly.

Advantages

2. Sorting can be done efficiently.

Disadvantages

1. Non economical and not eco friendly.
2. Time consuming process.

Experiment 5

To Determine the Peel Strength of a Given Samples

Objective

After performing this experiment you will be able to:

To determine the peel strength of a given samples.

Introduction

Packaging is a key element to quality branding for an organisation, ensuring that the product labels are securely attached to products. Adhesion bond strength of a film to a surface can be quantified in terms of peel strength, bonding strength, and shear strength. Many protective covers are used as required for various applications. In most of such applications plastics films are used as the first preference of the manufacturers. In applications like, protective LCD screens and other scratch-prone surfaces very low peel force films are used. The force required to remove the protective films or the label is very important for both the consumer and the manufacturer. For example, for protective film application, the film must be easy to remove, yet the bond must be strong enough to remain intact for product security. Whereas, in a typical adhesive application, like laminated cups, the bond between the surfaces should be strong enough to withstand various environmental impact.

In the packaging industry, peel strength testing measures the strength of seals between two flexible barrier materials. This measurement can then be used to determine consistency within the seal, in addition to the evaluation of the opening force of the package system. Seal strength is the quantitative measure for use in validation process, process control and capability. Seal strength is not only relevant to opening force and package integrity, but to measure the packaging processes ability to produce consistent seals.

Principle

Peel strength is generally used for the bond strength measurement of a material, typically an adhesive.

Peel strength is the required average load per unit width of bond line to separate bonded materials where the angle of separation is 180° (Fig. 1).

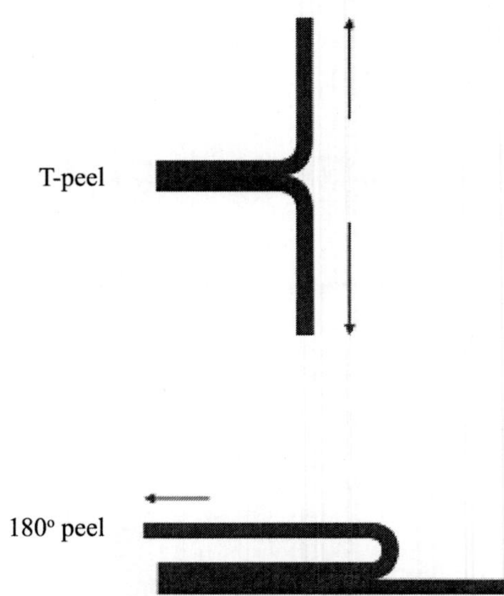

Fig. 1: Peel Test 90° and 180°

Procedure

Method I: ASTM D903-98 (2010) standard test method for stripping strength or peel strength of adhesive bonds where one flexible material is peeled off from a rigid surface. ASTM D903 is a common tensile test used to evaluate the peel or stripping characteristics of adhesively bonded materials used in a wide variety of applications in an even wider range of industries. Some examples of materials tested to ASTM D903 are plastic films, adhesive labels, and waterproofing materials.

1. To perform a test to ASTM D903, the adhesive materials must be cut into specimens 1" x 12" long. The specimens are then peeled away from either a flexible or rigid substrate at a 180° angle at a separation rate of 152.4 mm/min, or 6in/min. Test materials must be thick enough to withstand the expected tensile pull but not greater than 3 mm (1⁄8 in.) in thickness. Wherever possible, the standard thickness of specimens is: metals, 1.6 mm (1/16 in.); plastics, 1/16 in; wood, 1/8 in; rubber compounds, 1.9 mm (0.075 in.). If the flexible specimen is known to elongate when under load, it is important to use a more rigid substrate that is not expected to elongate under the same load.
2. Make sure your substrate is clean and dry, and then adhere six inches of your sample onto the substrate.
3. Place the specimen in the test machine by clamping one free end of the substrate in one grip. Now pull the free end of the specimen (such as a

strip of tape) over the back, in a "U" shape, and clamp it in the other grip. The specimen should now be in a "U" shape, and when pulled, will peel at a 180° angle (Fig. 2)

4. Set the machine at a rate of six inches per minute and pull at least one half of the specimen to measure the adhesive bond strength. Peel force is measured in pounds per inch (where inch is the length of the peel line).

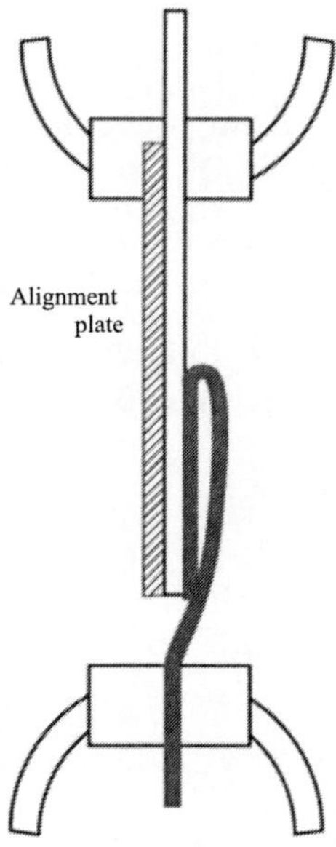

Fig. 2: ASTM D903 TEST METHOD (https://www.instron.com/en/testing-solutions/astm-standards/astm-d903#:~:text=ASTM%20D903%20is%20a%20common,adhesive%20labels%2C%20and%20waterproofing%20materials)

Method II:ASTM D6252- 90-degree peel test. (https://cdn.standards.iteh.ai/samples/13967/ebfef4f2e42941b4b8236042a9f1b2b2/ASTM-D6252-D6252M-98.pdf)

This test method covers the measurement of the peel adhesion of pressure-sensitive label stocks. This test method gives a measure of the adherence to a standard steel substrate or to other surfaces of interest for a pressure-sensitive label stock.

This test method provides a means of assessing the uniformity of the adhesion of a given type of pressure-sensitive label stock. The assessment may be within a sheet or roll, between sheets or rolls, or between production lots.

The sample should be approximately 150 mm in length. The specimens should be wider than 12.7 mm but narrower than 25.4 mm. If samples are in roll form, three to six outer wraps of label stock are thrown away.

1. First, make sure to clean the test plate with diacetone alcohol and dry it to get rid of any dirt or dust.
2. Place the specimen, release liner side up, and remove 5 to 6 inches of the release liner by pulling the release liner away from the adhesive and cutting to the appropriate length.
3. Next touch one end of the specimen with exposed adhesive to an end of the test panel. Hold the other end of the label up in the air so that it does not make contact with the panel.
4. Use a weighted roller and roll the label stock mechanically once in each direction, applying the label stock to the test panel.
5. Place the steel panel into the bottom fixture of the peel tester then clamp the free end of the specimen into the top grip.
6. Operate the adhesion tester at the separation speed outlined in the standard so that the sample is peeled off the test plate at a 90 degree angle.
7. Run peel tester at 12 in/min.

Observation

A typical graphical representation of load (in lb) vs. position (in inches) showing the maximum and minimum load required to peel off the sample to required distance. These values then can be used to infer the peel strength of the given sample.

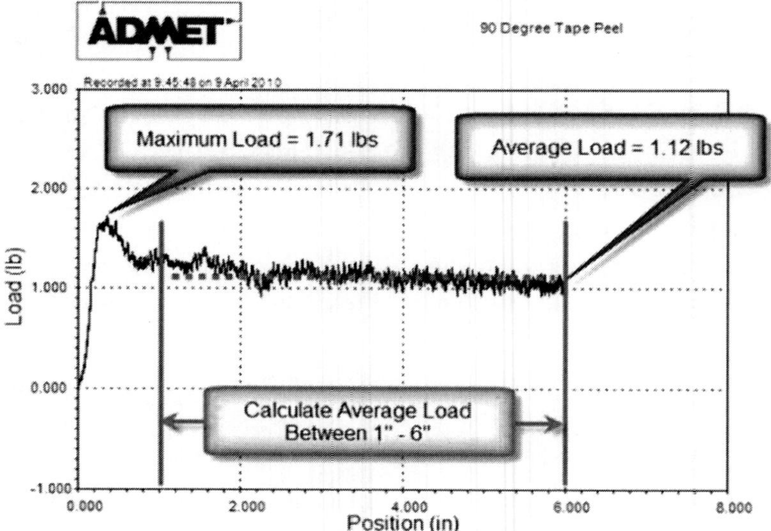

(*Source:* ADMET system Testing manufactures and materials)

There is a **first peak corresponding** to the force to begin opening the can. Then a tray with small variations which corresponds to the seal coat. Finally, a **last peak corresponding** to the force required to detach the end of the cap.

Inference

Sample	Load (in lb)	Position (in inches)	Peel Strength
1			
2			
3			
4			
Average			

Experiment 6

To Analyze the Stress-strain Curve of the Polymeric Film (Polystyrene) and Analyse the Curve

Objective

After performing this experiment you will be able to learn:

The stress-strain curve of the polymeric sample (polystyrene) and calculate the tensile strength, % elongation before break, young's modulus.

Principle

Tensile Test (ASTM D638)

Tensile strength is a measurement of ability of plastic material to withstand forces that tend to pull it apart. It is the amount of stress at the break point.

This test also helps to determine the extent the material stretches before breaking known as elongation at break. Percentage elongation is defined as the amount of linear deformation of the sample before breakage. It is measured as strain value at the break point.

Young's modulus is defined as the ratio between stress and strain at a point (Hooke's law must be obeyed).

Y = Stress/Strain

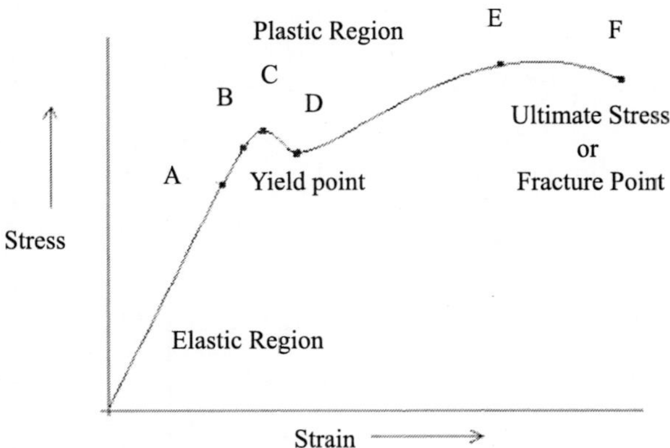

(*Source:* https://en.wikipedia.org/wiki/Stress–strain_curve)

Yield Point: It is the point at which an increase in strain occurs on stress-strain curve without the increase in stress. (point C)

Yield Strength: The stress at which a specified limiting deviation from the proportionality of stress-strain curve is observed for a material is known as Yeild strength.

Proportional Limit: It is defined as the maximum stress at which a material is can sustain the applied load without any deviation from the proportionality of stress-strain curve (point B).

Ultimate Strength: The maximum stress a material will tolerate when subjected to an applied load .

Procedure

ASTM D882 is a common method of examining the mechanical properties of thin plastic films of less than 1 mm (0.040 in).

In this test, a sample of film is mounted between two grips that are 250 mm (10 in) apart at the beginning of the test (gage length) distance which are then pulled by applying a tensile load. The elongation (or extension) produced in the sample is registered as the load increases.

If your plastic samples are thicker than 1 mm (0.04 in) you should consider **ASTM D638.**

ASTM D882 stretches a specimen until it fails. Plastic films and sheeting are typically highly elastic, and this means that the sample is to be tested at a high crosshead speeds, based on the criteria in the standard.

In order to calculate the required crosshead speed, multiply the starting length of the specimen (distance between grips) by the starting strain rate in mm/mm per min.

Preparation of film

a) Polystyrene granules are dissolved in a 10 ml toluene solvent at 70 degree Celsius.

b) After the clear solution is obtained the solution is casted to a flat surface.

c) The film obtained after solvent evaporation is cut into specific dimension which is ready for test.

Sample	Thickness average (mm)	Width (mm)	Length (cm)	Area (mm^2)
1				
2				
3				
4				

Testing

The sample is clamped into a UTM and the start button is pushed. The clamps start pulling the sample apart along with plotting the stress-strain curve simultaneously. The specimen breaks at some point and the graph is analyzed.

Observation

Sample	Final Length (cm)	Change in Length (cm)	Force (N)	Stress (N/Mm²)	Stress (MPa)	Strain	Young Modulus (MPa)	% Elongation
1								
2								
3								
4								

Results

Tensile strength = ………. MPa

% elongation = ….. %

Young's modulus = ……… N/m^2

Ultimate yield strength = …….. MPa.

Inference

Experiment 7

To Determine the Tensile Properties of Polymeric Sample

Objective

After performing this experiment you will be able to learn:

To determine the tensile properties of polymeric sample.

Principle

ASTM D638 covers the tensile properties of both reinforced and unreinforced plastics in the form of dumbbell-shaped molded plastic test specimens.

This test method uses standard "dumbell" or "dogbone" shaped specimens of rigid plastic samples between 1 to 14 mm (0.03 to 0.55 in) then ASTM D638

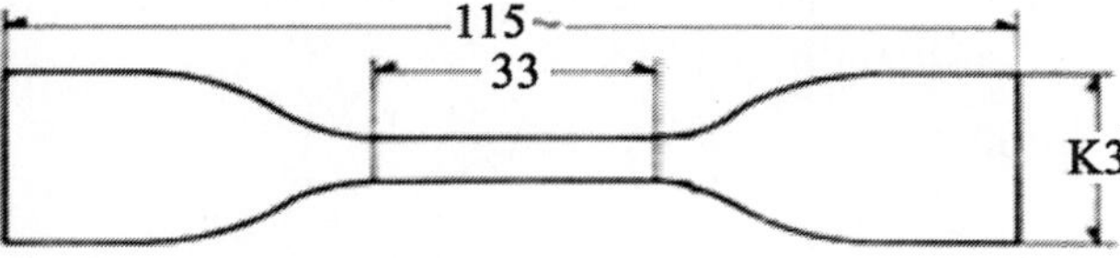

Theory

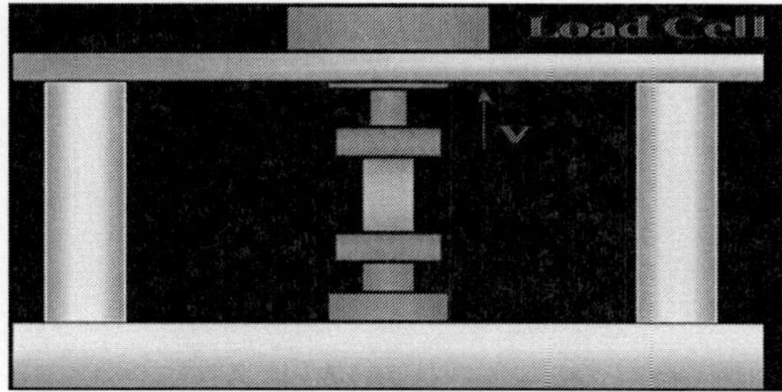

The test method is according to ASTM D638

Tensile Yield Strength

Yield strength is measured as the highest stress where a film, when deformed, will resume its original dimensions when the force is removed. The yield stress is expressed as force per unit area (engineering stress) and is calculated as per Equation (1) and the elongation at yield as per equation (2).

Equation (1) $\sigma_y = F_y / (\text{width} * \text{thickness})$, psi (MPa)

Equation (2) $\varepsilon_y = L_y / (L_o) * 100\%$

Ultimate Tensile Strength

Ultimate tensile strength is the measurement of the force per area where the film ruptured as shown in Equation (3). The ultimate tensile strength can be used to calculate the relative strength of the sample. Sample thickness is considered in the calculation of ultimate tensile strength, however it is strongly influenced by orientation of the polymer chains. Hence the valuesof ultimate tensile strength can vary significantly even at the same film thickness. Better unidirectional orientation in a film increases the ultimate tensile strength of a film. Higher molecular weight and narrow MWD produce higher tensile strength.

Equation (3) $\sigma_T = F_T / (\text{width} * \text{thickness})$, psi (MPa)

Ultimate Elongation

Ultimate elongation is a measurement of deformation per unit length where the sample gets ruptured as shown in Equation (4). Ultimate Elongation is strongly influenced by chain orientation and molecular weight. Hence, the values vary significantly even at the same film thickness. Increasing orientation in a sample will increase the ultimate tensile strength of a film.

Equation (4) $\varepsilon_T = L_T / (L_o) * 100\ \%$

Secant Modulus

The elastic region is related to the stiffness/flexibility of the sample and is referred to as the secant modulus. It may be determined by the ratio of force to strain at either 1% or 2% elongation and reported as psi (MPa).

Toughness

The tensile toughness is defined as the area under the stress-strain curve. The results are reported as ft-lb_f/in^3 (J/cm^3).

Procedure

1. Cut or injection mold your material into one of the five "dumbbell" shapes. The exact shape you use is dependent upon your material's rigidity and thickness.
2. Typically a sample has a thickness of 3.2 mm (0.125 in) and a gauge length of 50 mm (2 in).
3. Using the universal test machine, the specimen is placed between two clamps or grips with the edges of the specimen parallel to the direction of

the load. The specimen grips are tightened to hold the specimen securely within the fixture.

4. The test specimen is then pulled apart at tensile rates ranging from speeds from 1 to 500 mm/min (0.3 to 19.6 in/min) until it breaks.
5. End the test after sample break (rupture)

Observation

The equipment used for this test, that is **UTM** is a fully automatic machine. it gives the observation and result of all the mechanical properties in the following manner.

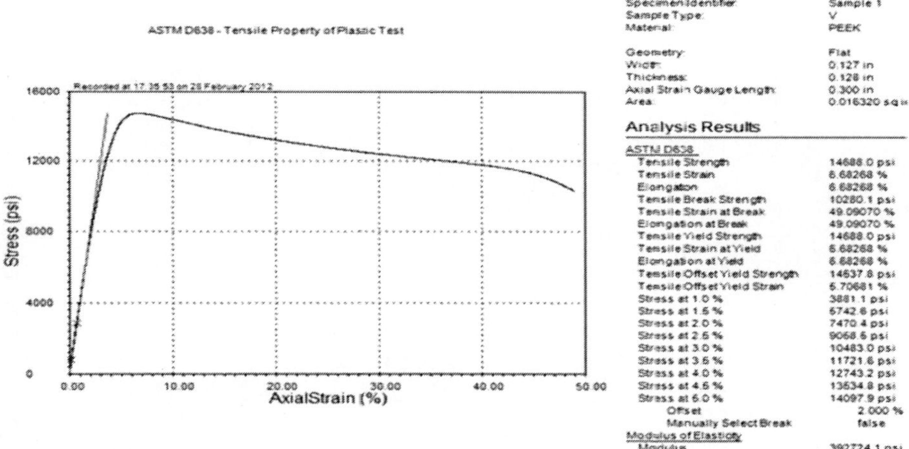

(*Source:* Wikipedia)

Calculation

Tensile strength is calculated by dividing the load at break by the original minimum cross-sectional area. The result is expressed in megapascals (MPa) and reported to three significant figures.

Tensile strength = (load at break) / (original width) x (original thickness)

Inference

1. Tensile Yield Strength =
2. Ultimate Tensile Strength =
3. Elongation =
4. Poisson's Ratio =

Experiment 8

To Determine the Tear Resistance of Polymeric Film

Objective

After performing this experiment you will be able to learn:

To determine the tear resistance of polymeric film.

Introduction

Tear resistance testing is often used in the plastic film, paper and textile industries. Tear resistance is measured as a sample's ability to resist tearing. Tear strength is the maximum london the sample divided by the thickness of the material. Typically used for testing of plastic film, plastic sheets and other rubber products. Tear strength is calculated by force (in Newtons) divided by thickness (in millimeters, centimeters, inches, etc.): Tear strength = F/t

A tear is generally uneven and usually unplanned. In cases like a packaged chips, already tear cuts are made following a perforated line so that the effort of tearing is less and the action will most likely produce a straight line.

The speed at which a tear resistance test is conducted can affect the test significantly. Tear transmission resistance is common for acceptance testing with materials such as paper and rubber. Tear resistance in textiles involves the load required to spread a single "rip-tongue" type of tear or the type of tear where the material is initially cut.

Materials vary in their vulnerability to tearing. Some materials may be quite resistant to tearing when they are in their full form, but when a small cut or tear is made, the resistance is compromised, and the effort needed to continue tearing along that line becomes less.

Principle

ASTM D1004-13 reports the maximum tear resistance in units of force (lbf or N) and the maximum extension in units of length (in or mm). The specimen must be die-cut to specifications found in the standard. Specimens are formed with a 90° notch to create a stress concentration in a specific area which will initiate a tear. The specimen is then subjected to a tensile test at 2 in/min (51 mm/min) until complete failure. The specimen geometry and test speed are not intended to simulate real world tear conditions; instead, ASTM D1004 is intended to create a controlled tear off to analyze force versus displacement data for quality control or material comparison purposes.

ASTM D1004 is not applicable for plastic material where brittle failure occurs or where elongation greater than 200% occurs. Material between those two extremes has been shown to reliably use ASTM D1004 to compare tear resistance between materials.

The resistance to tear of plastic film and sheeting, while partly dependent upon thickness, has no simple correlation with specimen thickness. Hence, tearing forces measured in newtons (or pounds-force) cannot be normalized over a wide range of specimen thickness without producing misleading data as to the actual tearing resistance of the material. Data from this test method are comparable only from specimens, which vary by no more than ±10 % from the nominal or average thickness of all specimens tested. Therefore, the tearing resistance is expressed in maximum newtons (or pounds-force) of force to tear the specimen.

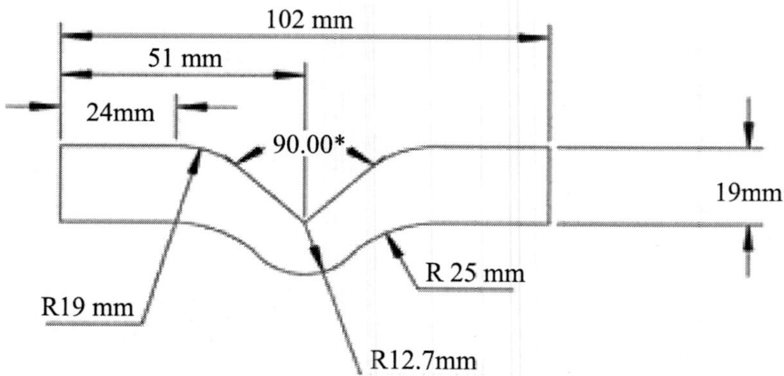

(https://www.astm.org/d1004-21.html)

Procedure

1. This test method covers the determination of the tear resistance of flexible plastic film and sheeting at very low rates of loading, 51 mm (2 in.)/min. and is designed to measure the force to initiate tearing.
2. The specimen geometry of this test method produces a stress concentration in a small area of the specimen. The maximum stress, usually found near the onset of tearing, is recorded as the tear resistance in newtons (or pounds-force).

3. The method is not applicable for film or sheeting material where brittle failures occur during testing or where maximum extension is greater than 101.6 mm (4 in.).
4. Although resistance to tear can be expressed in newtons per microns, (pounds-force per mil) of specimen thickness, this is only advisable where correlation for the particular material being tested has been established. In most cases, comparison between films of dissimilar thickness is not valid.

Observation

Sample	Conditioned/Non-conditioned	Tear strength	% decrease

Calculation

Tear strength is calculated by force (in Newtons) divided by thickness (in millimeters, centimeters, inches, etc.):

Tear strength = F/t

Inference

Tearing force in milli-newtons (or gms-force) =

Experiment 9

To Determine the Impact Properties of Polymeric Film

Objective

After performing this experiment you will be able to learn:

The impact properties of polymeric film.

Introduction

Dart impact test is performed on plastic films and laminates to determine the effect of free falling dart on plastic films. The energy created by the falling dart causes the film to fail under some specified conditions. The test is widely performed by the manufacturers in plastic industries and paper & packaging industries to assess the durability and strength of the plastic films and other related products.

Dart impact strength is dependent on film thickness as the test is sensitive to orientation of the chains in the film. The tackiness of the film (slip additives) and the condition of the dart surface also influence the values determined by this test. As dart impact is not tested in any specific film direction, it is sensitive to chain orientation in both directions. Best impact strength are usually obtained when the orientation is balanced in the Machine Direction and Cross Direction.

Principle

The test method is according to ASTM D1709

There are two methods used in drop dart impact testing:

Method A drops the dart from a height of 26 inches (660 mm) above the film sample. The values will typically range between 40 grams and 1400 grams. This method works well for thin films (< 3 mils or < 75 microns).

Method B drops the dart from a height of 60 inches (1524 mm). This method is used for thick films or films with very low crystallinity.

The values from the two methods (A or B) can not be converted to the other method.

Impact Resistance = M_{100} – D (S1/100 – 0.5)

Where,

M_{100} = Lowest weight according to the D used at which 100% failure occurs.

D = Uniform increment weight used (in grams)

S1 = Result (Percentage Failure) – Sum of Percentage of breaks at each weight.

Procedure

- Select appropriate weight of the dart, which is nearest to the expected impact failure weight.
- You can also add required number of incremental weights to the dart shaft and put the locking collar in its place in order to set the weights in a particular location.
- Place the first test sample from the top of the clamp ensuring that it is uniformly flat and wrinkle free and overlaps the clamp by about 25 mm on all sides. Hold the sample firmly. Put on the vacuum pump to adjust the sample to get stretched and for the wrinkle free and fold free sample.

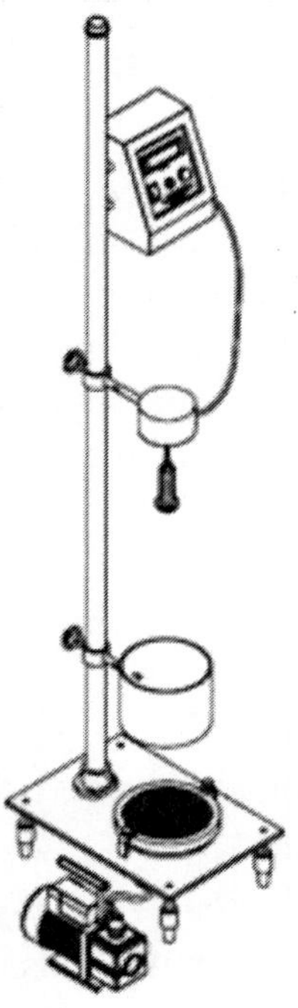

- After the sample is held firmly in the clamp, place the upper tip of dart in the center hole of the electromagnet and keep it pressed in an upward direction.

How to take the exact reading of the Scale?

To perform the test, fix the electromagnet clamp / holder at different length of 660 mm & 1524 mm with the given formula:

Scale Length + Dart Length + Electro Magnet length = Reading of Scale

For example:

1. If the length of scale is 660, 660 mm + 212 mm + 35 mm = 907 mm
2. If the length of the scale is 1524 mm, 1524 mm + 226 mm + 35 mm = 1785 mm

- Now press the push button on the side of the channel to activate the electromagnet.
- Now release the push button to enable the dart to fall on the centre of the specimen which is held in the clamp.
- Examine the test sample to determine whether it has failed or not.

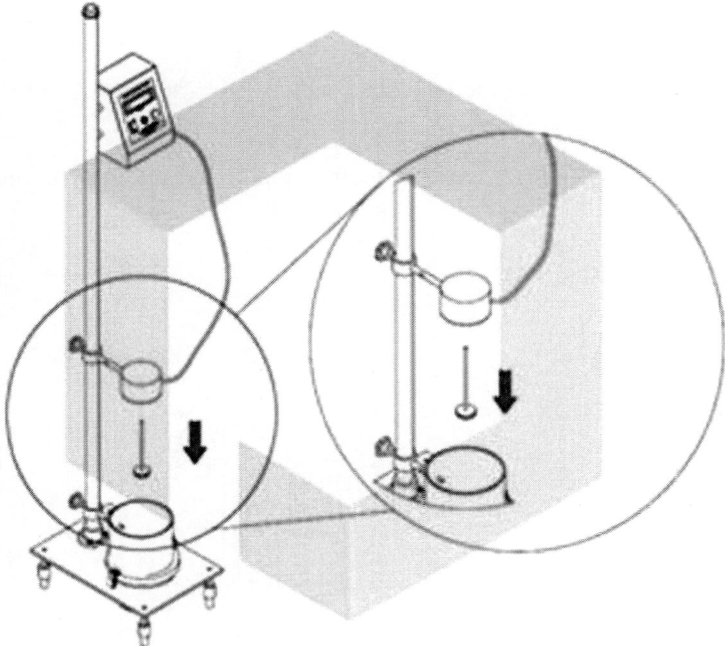

- If the sample failed, reduce down the weight and if not failed, then take fresh test sample to perform the test with the enhanced weight.

  i) Repeat the process until the sample fails at least 50%

Observation

Sample Results are given below

Weight (gms)	No. of Test Samples Taken	Result (Percentage Failure)	Number of Samples Broken

Observation Table

Impact Failure Weight = ... Grams

Calculation:

Impact Resistance = M_{100} – D (S1/100 – 0.5)

Where,

M_{100} = lowest weight according to the D used at which 100% failure occurs.

D = Uniform increment weight used (in grams)

S1 = Result (Percentage Failure) – Sum of Percentage of breaks at each weight.

Inference

1. Impact failure weight (gms) =
2. Impact resistance =

Experiment 10

To Analyze the Compatibility of Food Packaging Materials Using Shelf-life Studies

Objective

After performing this experiment you will be able to learn:

The procedure to analysethe Compatibility of Food Packaging Materials Using Shelf- Life.

Introduction

When testing a food product for shelf-life and stability, the packaging is a major factor to be considered. It is necessary to carry out stability testing in the packaging intended for marketing due to interactions that may occur between the package, the product and the environment. Testing is also important for establishing the correct specifications for procurement and quality control of incoming materials.

The standards of packaging materials play a significant role in establishing optimum packaging specification. Properties of packaging materials like plastic and paper are affected by variables like temperature and humidity. Sensitivity of the packaging material to heat, light and moisture is due to their chemical nature. Compatibility of the packaging is as significant as development of the packaging systems or selecting packaging materials for food products.

Principle

Shelf-life prediction is required when the package is permeable or semi-permeable to atmospheric agents like water-vapor or/and oxygen. Metal containers, glass bottles, aluminium foil are used mainly for their absolute barrier against moisture vapor and gases. However, compatibility of metal containers with specific food items need to be ascertained and wherever necessary, suitable lacquer coatings may need to be provided to achieve product-package compatibility. The lining materials/wads of the closures/caps in glass jars also should be compatible with the packed food product.

Though polymeric packaging materials are not absolute barriers against moisture vapor and gases, they have been found to be increasingly useful due to various advantages like light weight, easy to carry, easy to transport, handle and stock. The most important function of the package is to contain the product and provide protection against changes in quality caused by adverse effects of surrounding environment. The selected packaging material has to be compatible with the product to be packed and should provide specific protection to maintain shelf-life i.e. quality preservation as well as economic considerations and competitive packaging. All these are taken into consideration in design and selection of a packaging system.

Shelf-life studies can be carried out by actually packing the freshly manufactured product in different packing materials (selected for the study) and exposing adequate number of packages to different climatic conditions or to accelerated and standard conditions For the purpose of creating the storage conditions, humidity cabinets or environmental walk-in-chambers are used. For average Indian climates are generally taken as:

Walk in Climatic Chamber

- Standard Condition: 27°C ± 1°C, 65% ± 2% R.H.
- Accelerated Conditions: 38°C ± 2°C, 90% ± 2% R.H.

During the exposure period, the packages are withdrawn at fixed intervals of time to assess the quality of the product as per the product quality attributes. This is continued till the product becomes commercially unacceptable i.e. degradation occurs of the primary product quality attribute.The results obtained on the assessment of the product quality and the packages are analyzed for overall acceptability. Based on the analysis, shelf-life of the product in a particular package is analyzed which ultimately determines the product-package compatibility.

Procedure

i) Select different packaging materials for analyzing product-package compatibility.

ii) Package freshly manufactured product in the selected packaging materials.

iii) Expose the packages to standard and accelerated climatic conditions.

iv) Withdraw each package (packaging materials selected for study) at fixed intervals of time and assess the quality of the product as per primary quality attributes.

v) Continue the shelf-life study till the product gets degraded and become unacceptable.

Observation

- Quality assessment of the product in various packaging materials at standard conditions:

S. No.	Packaging Material	Duration	Weight	Appearance	Color	Flavor	Texture	Overall accepta-bility
1.		0 Day						
		7 Days						
		14 Days						
		21 Days						
		28 Days						
		35 Days						
2.		0 Day						
		7 Days						
		14 Days						
		21 Days						
		28 Days						
		35 Days						
3.		0 Day						
		7 Days						
		14 Days						
		21 Days						
		28 Days						
		35 Days						

- Quality assessment of the product in various packaging materials at accelerated conditions:

S. No.	Packaging Material	Duration	Weight	Appearance	Color	Flavor	Texture	Overall acceptability
1.		0 Day						
		7 Days						
		14 Days						
		21 Days						
		28 Days						
		35 Days						
2.		0 Day						
		7 Days						
		14 Days						
		21 Days						
		28 Days						
		35 Days						
3.		0 Day						
		7 Days						
		14 Days						
		21 Days						
		28 Days						
		35 Days						

Inference

Experiment 11

To Determine the Caliper / GSM of Paperboard

Objective

After performing this experiment you will be able to learn:

How to determine the caliper/GSM of paperboard.

Introduction

Thickness is calculated as the perpendicular distance between the two principle surfaces of paper or paperboard as measured under specified conditions. The GSM of paper may be defined as the thickness of a paper that is measured in a roundabout way. GSM stands for Gms per Square Metre - and is used to check the quality of the paper to be measured.

It is a very simple to perform test but tells a lot about the basic properties of the material which are very important to decide the quality of the material. Also, the quality of the material is measured with its GSM value. The heavier a paperboard is, the better the quality.

Principle

Packaging materials are chosen by estimating the GSM of the sample material. High Grammage defines the strength of the paper. In certain applications high Grammage is desired, where the paper will be subjected to load and harsh working conditions.

Thickness is an important property of most grades of paper and paperboard as it affects density, air resistance, rigidity and many other important properties. For many end use requirements, a low level of thickness variation is necessary in addition to meeting the average thickness specified. The thickness of book paper controls the thickness of the finished book and also affects the opacity. The electrical insulation efficiency of capacitor paper is directly related to the square of the thickness. Newsprint, linerboard, tabulating cards, blotting paper, printing papers, and many other paper grades require thickness uniformity for subsequent processing or performance.

GSM Grammage tester measures the weight of the substrate of a particular dimension. This test is the basis test for all paper and paperboard related industries, which determines the quality of the substrate. Commonly only the paper which has more grammage is suitable for printing. Paper which has more grammage has more strike through and hence the spreading of the inks is controlled. This also ensures the quality end product. The properties and life of the packaged product may be enhanced by choosing the right GSM of paper. For packaging related materials, it is necessary to have more grammage. The weight of the substrate in one square meter is termed as GSM – GSM per square meter.

The thickness of any pressure sensitive material is measured with the help of a dead weight dial type micrometer gauge. The Thickness Gauge (Dead Weight type) is a bench-model instrument. It consists of a rigid cast aluminum base and arm on which a dial indicator is held firmly. The dial indicator has a flat circular pressure foot, which exerts a specified pressure on the specimen kept on an anvil.

The pressure foot of the micrometer automatically lifts up and comes down on an inserted sample. During the upstroke of the instrument, the sample is placed between the jaws of the micrometer. Wait for the pressure foot to come down and quickly make a reading just before it lifts up again. The thickness reading is affected by the moisture content of the sample so the test shall be made on samples and in an atmosphere both conditioned.

Extremely thin papers are measured using a specimen of several sheets between the micrometer surfaces.

Procedure

1. Obtain a sample of the paper /paper board from the stock.
2. Condition the paper before testing. Measure the thickness by placing the sample between the anvil and pressure foot of the Micrometer/thickness gauge.
3. Note down the reading in mm and remove the sample.
4. Now cut the sample according to the given template (20 x 25 cm^2) for carrying the GSM test.
5. Before placing the sample ensure that pointer reading shows zero.
6. Place the sample in the given basket of GSM tester and note down the pointer reading.
7. Remove the sample and mark both the readings.

Inference

Thickness and Grammage of the given sample is determined by using Thickness gauge and quadrant scale.

Experiment 12

To Calculate the Burst Strength of the Given Paper and Board

Objective

After performing this experiment you will be able to:

Calculate the Burst strength of the given paper and Board.

Introduction

Bursting strength is defined as the measure of resistance to rupture in various materials. A test specimen is held between two circular clamps and subjected to an increasing pressure from a rubber diaphragm. The rubber diaphragm keeps on expanding with the help of a controlled pneumatic pressure until the test specimen ruptures. The pressure required to rupture the specimen at the time of reading is known as bursting strength.

Principle

The bursting strength of paper, paper board, including linerboard and corrugated board, is a combined measure of properties of the sheet, like tensile strength and elongation. In general, bursting strength is dependent on the type, proportion, preparation and amount of fibres present in the sheet and their formation, internal sizing, and to some degree, the surface treatment. Since bursting strength is an empirical property, this test serves to define "standard grades" in commercial activity in combination with basis weight.

Recommended for paper, Paperboard, Corrugated board, Nonwovens, Textiles, Geo-textiles, Film, Tissue, Tobacco Leaf etc.

Procedure

1. Obtain the required size of sample approximately 30 mm dia.
2. Hold the sample between the annular circular clamps.
3. Now apply sufficient pressure by hand wheel to firmly hold the sample.
4. Switch on the pressure button and wait until the sample gets bursted.
5. Stop the pressure switch and note down the reading from the dial.
6. Remove the sample from annular circular clamps.

Inference

This test determines the amount of Hydrostatic pressure required to rupture the given material.

Experiment 13

Determination of Water Absorption of Packaging Material by COBB Method

Objective

After performing this experiment you will be able to learn:

The water absorption of packaging material by Cobb method.

Introduction

The water absorptive capacity, or Cobb value, is defined as the mass of water absorbed in a specific time by 1 square meter of paper, board, or corrugated fiberboard under a head of 1 cm of water. To determine this value, conditioned test pieces are weighed before and after being exposed to water under specified conditions. The excess water is removed using blotting paper and a brass roller of defined dimensions and weight. The test piece is weighed immediately before and after exposure to water for a specified duration on one surface. The increase in mass due to water absorption is expressed in grams per square meter (g/m^2).

The Cobb value defines the water absorbency of paper as the amount of water absorbed by one side of a unit area of paper or board placed horizontally under a 1 cm water head within a given time.

Principle

This method, developed by Cobb, measures the amount of water absorbed by paper, paperboard, or corrugated fiberboard over a specified period under standardized conditions. It is applicable to paper or board that is not fully penetrated by water during the selected absorption time.

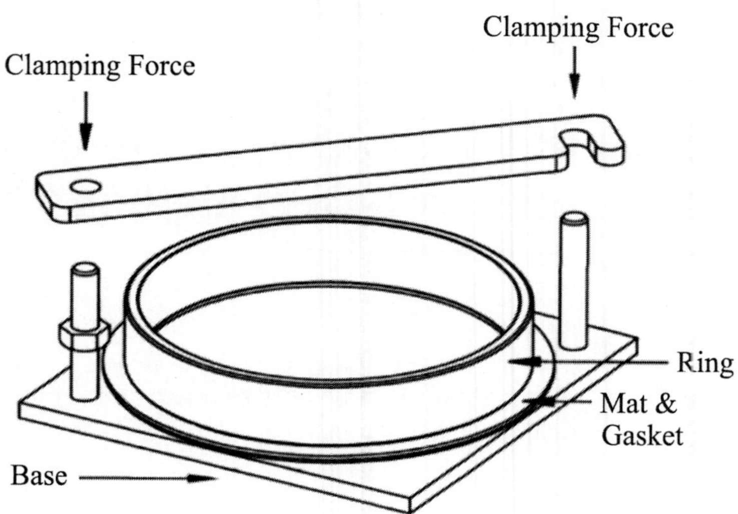

Specimen holder

Theory: The Cobb test assesses the water absorption capacity of the outer surface of sized paper, paperboard, or corrugated fiberboard over a defined period, typically 60 or 180 seconds (referred to as Cobb60 or Cobb180). The result is expressed in grams per square meter (g/m^2). Water absorbency can significantly impact properties such as printability and the setting rate of water-based adhesives.

The Cobb test determines the quantity of water absorbed by the surface of paper or board in a given time. Water absorption is influenced by characteristics like sizing and porosity. This test is critical for certain certifications, including those related to hazardous material packaging, and can be used to evaluate various hygroscopic surfaces designed to resist water absorption. However, it is not intended for the precise assessment of the writing properties of paper, although it provides a general indication of suitability for use with aqueous inks. Sizing and absorption properties are essential for writing and printing quality and the material's appearance after handling and practical use.

Procedure

1. Cut Test Pieces: Prepare test pieces with dimensions of 140 mm x 140 mm. Ensure the pieces are free from folds, wrinkles, or other defects not inherent in the material.
2. Weigh Test Pieces: Accurately weigh each test piece.
3. Position on Rubber Mat: Place the test piece on a dry rubber mat on the baseboard and clamp it in position under a dry, clean cylinder to prevent water leakage between the cylinder and the sample during testing.

4. Prepare Water: Pour 100 mL of distilled water at 27°C into the measuring cylinder. This will create a 1 cm head of water.
5. Select Absorption Time: Set the absorption time to 60 seconds.
6. Start the Test: Once the set time has elapsed, immediately remove the cylinder, taking care to keep the dry areas of the test piece free from contact with water.
7. Blot the Test Piece: Place the test piece with the wetted side up on a sheet of blotting paper on a flat, rigid surface.
8. Blotting Procedure: At the end of the selected absorption time, cover the test piece with a second sheet of blotting paper and roll the brass roller back and forth over the pad without applying extra pressure.
9. Final Weighing: Fold the test piece with its dry side facing outward and weigh it immediately to prevent weight loss due to evaporation

X = 100 (A - B)/area

A = weight of test pieces after wetting (in gm)

B = weight of test pieces before wetting (in gm)

X = water absorbing COBB value (in gm/meter square)

Observation

Inference

Experiment 14

To Calculate the Scuff Resistance of the Printed Sample

Objective

After performing this experiment you will be able to learn :

The Scuff Resistance of the Printed Sample.

Introduction

Scuff resistance or abrasion resistance is a desirable and sometimes critical property of printed materials. Abrasion damage can occur during shipment, storage, handling, and end use. The result is a significant decrease in product appearance and legibility of product information. A printed substrate's level of abrasion damage is influenced by numerous factors, including time, temperature, humidity, and shipping circumstances. This procedure offers a means of comparing printed materials' resistance to scuffs in a lab setting. The relative scuff resistance of printed inks, coatings, laminates, and substrates can also be assessed using this technique. This procedure can be changed to assess how a product—food, drink, powdered detergent, etc.—affects scuff resistance, which might happen when something spills or leaks while being transported. Labels, folding cartons, corrugated boxes, circulars, inserts, and other packaging materials with applied graphics on a flat substrate can all use this technique.

Principle

Depending on which weight is being used, the test specimen is mounted on top of the rubber pad on the Sutherland base, and the receptor is cut to fit either the 0.91 kg (2-lb) or 1.81 kg (4-lb) weight. The weight is fixed to the receptor. The number of strokes (one back-and-forth cycle) the sample is rubbed determines how long the test will take. The Timer has a predefined number of strokes that can be used. After mounting the weight on the Sutherland, the machine is powered on. When the predetermined amount of strokes is reached, the Sutherland will turn itself off automatically. The test specimen is removed from the base and examined for degree of print degradation. The receptor is analyzed for the amount of ink transferred from the specimen. Results are compared to an agreed upon standard sample tested in the identical fashion.

Procedure

1. Mount a 76 by 152 mm (3 by 6 in.) rubber pad 3 both on top of the base as well as to the bottom face of the detectable receptor block.
2. Mount the receptor to the rubber pad of the receptor block with pressure sensitive tape, outside the test area [only if using the 51 by 102 mm (2 by 4 in.) receptor].
3. Attach the test specimen to the rubber pad on the base with the test surface face exposed.
4. Attach the receptor to the receptor block. The 51 by 178 mm (2 by 5 in.) The receptor is held in place by the clamps on the sides of the block, while the 51 by 102 mm (2 by 4 in.) The receptor is held in place by the pressure-sensitive tape.
5. Lightly brush the sample and receptor with a camel's hair anti-static brush to remove any potentially abrasive particles from the surface.
6. Place the receptor block in the receptor block holder.
7. Preset the dial on the Rub Tester to the desired number of strokes.
8. Turn them on. It will automatically shut off when the preset number of strokes has been completed.
9. Repeat 1 to 8 with each test specimen. Repeat 1 to 8 with the reference standard.

Evaluation of sample

Examine each specimen for degree of degradation and each receptor for the amount of material transferred from the print.

Report test conditions and results for abrasion using predetermined criteria established by the interested parties.

Observation

S No.	Sample specimen	Receptor no.	No. of strokes	Extent of degradation

Inference

Experiment 15

To Perform Gas/ Vacuum Packaging of Foods and Study their Shelf Life Studies

Objective

After performing this experiment you will be able to learn:

Gas / Vacuum packaging of foods and study their shelf life studies.

Introduction

Vacuum packaging is a food preservation technique that removes air from the package before sealing. This method involves manually or automatically placing items in a plastic film package, extracting the air, and sealing the package. The primary goal of vacuum packaging is to remove oxygen from the container to extend the shelf life of foods and, in the case of flexible packages, to reduce the volume of the contents and package. Shrink films are sometimes used to create a tight fit around the contents. Vacuum packaging is commonly used to store dry foods like cereals, nuts, cured meats, cheese, and coffee for extended periods. For short-term storage, vacuum packaging can also be used for fresh foods, such as vegetables and liquids, as it inhibits bacterial growth.

Shelf Life Studies

The food and consumer products industries use shelf life studies to determine and validate how long a product retains its quality under specific storage conditions. This information is crucial to ensure the safety and quality of products before they reach consumers. During a product's shelf life, it must:

Be safe to use

Retain the expected quality traits characteristic of the product

Meet any nutritional claims indicated on the label

Companies often seek shelf life studies from EMSL, which offers both real-time and accelerated studies based on the client's needs.

Advantages of Vacuum Packaging

Eliminates oxidation

Prevents evaporation of volatile components

Preserves delicate flavors and oils

Prevents freezer burn by protecting food from exposure to cold, dry air

Maintains natural moisture

Extends shelf life

Reduces the bulk of non-food items (e.g., clothing and bedding can be stored in vacuum-sealed bags).

Types of Vacuum Packaging Machines

- External Bag Machine: Only the ends of the bag fit into the machine, while the rest of the bag and its contents remain outside.
- Vacuum Chamber Machine: The entire bag, along with its contents, fits inside the machine and is then sealed.

Principle of Vacuum Chamber Machine

- Evacuation: Air is extracted from the vacuum chamber by a vacuum pump, evacuating both the bag and the product.
- MAP Function (Optional): The chamber and bag are filled with a protective gas until the desired pressure is reached, further extending shelf life and preserving fresh color (e.g., for meat).
- Sealing: An electrical impulse heats the sealing wire, melting the sealable inner sides of the bag and closing it.
- Ventilation: Air flows back into the chamber. For sensitive products, a soft-air ventilation option provides extra protection against deformation due to air pressure. Once the internal and external pressures are equalized, the chamber lid opens, and the vacuum-packed product can be removed.

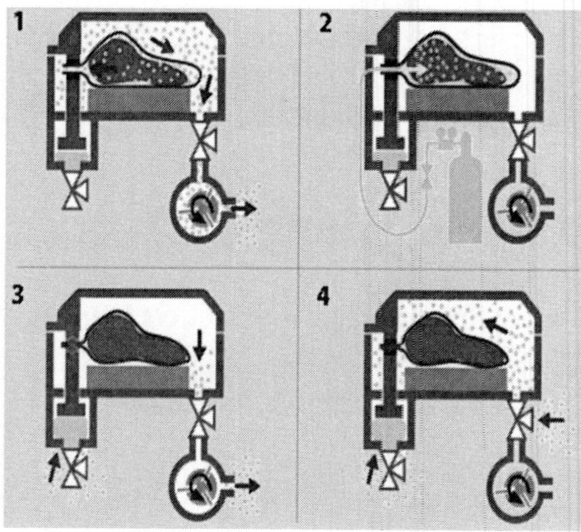

Procedure

- Use a weighing scale to measure 200 grams of peanuts.
- Preheat the oven to 180°C.
- Lightly coat the peanuts with a small amount of oil.
- Spread the peanuts evenly on a baking tray.
- Roast the peanuts in the oven for 20 minutes or until they turn golden brown.
- Allow the roasted peanuts to cool completely.
- Divide the roasted peanuts into four 50-gram portions.
- Place each portion in a separate plastic or aluminum packet, ensuring one packet is designated as the control sample.
- Place three packets in a vacuum chamber for vacuum packaging.
- Heat seal the control packet without vacuum packaging.
- Store all four packets under the same conditions: 37°C temperature and 60% humidity.
- Periodically examine the packets for flavor and sensory attributes at 7, 14, 21, and 28 days.
- Record the observations using a hedonic scal.

Hedonic Scale

This test measures the level of liking for food products by a population and is used to assess product presence or acceptance. Panelists are asked to evaluate each sample and mark their preferences on a scale. Hedonic scale ratings are converted to numerical scores, and statistical analysis is applied to determine differences in the degree of liking between or among samples. This is also known as the nine-point hedonic scale.

Inference

Use this scale to indicate your attitude toward the sample by checking the point that best describes your feeling:

1. Dislike Extremely
2. Dislike Very much
3. Dislike Moderately
4. Dislike slightly
5. Neither Like Nor dislike
6. Like slightly

7. Like Moderately
8. Like Very much
9. Like Extremely

Time Period (Days)	Appearance	Color	Flavor	Taste	Overall Acceptability
0					
7					
14					
21					
28					

Experiment 16

Special Quality Assurance Needs Good Manufacturing Practices, HACCP, Validation Protocols, etc.

Objective

After performing this experiment you will be able to learn:

Special quality assurance needs, good manufacturing practices, HACCP, validation protocols, etc.

Introduction

Packaging is a very important element in product quality maintenance that is why quality of packaging has great influence and its quality assurance is necessary. Physical flow in the supply chain may deteriorate some packaging features, so their monitoring and proper conditions of storage, transport and suitable protection are important.

The quality of packaging is essential; it is an important element of product quality and supply chain effectiveness. Packaging is influenced by quality of raw materials, proper conduct of the production, storage, transport and distribution processes in a company. That is why a lot of companies implement quality assurance or management systems. In regards to packaging risk categories there are different requirements.

The most important requirements in respective to food packaging is that materials shall be manufactured in compliance with good manufacturing practice so that, under normal or foreseeable conditions of use, they do not transfer their constituents to food in quantities which could: endanger human health, bring about an unacceptable change in the composition of the food and bring about a deterioration in the organoleptic characteristics thereof (Regulation (EC) No 1935/2004). Moreover the packaging labeling, advertising and presentation shall not mislead the consumers. Regulation also state that (Regulation (EC) No 1935/2004):

- The traceability of packaging materials shall be ensured at all stages in order to facilitate control, the recall of defective products, consumer information and the attribution of responsibility.

- Business operators shall have in place systems and procedures to allow identification of the businesses from which and to which materials are supplied.
- The materials which are placed on the market shall be identifiable by an appropriate system which allows their traceability by means of labeling or relevant documentation or information.

Commission Regulation (EC) No 2023/2006 of 22 December 2006 on good manufacturing practice for materials and articles intended to come into contact with food requires the business operator shall establish, implement and ensure adherence to an effective and documented quality assurance system. Quality assurance system is understood as: "the total sum of the organized and documented arrangements made with the purpose of ensuring that materials and articles are of the quality required to ensure conformity with the rules applicable to them and the quality standards necessary for their intended use" (Commission Regulation (EC) No 2023/2006).

The packaging sector operators should implement proper quality control systems, which ensure effective quality control and ensure monitoring of the implementation and achievement of Good Manufacturing Practice (GMP) and identify measures to correct any failure to achieve GMP. Such corrective measures shall be implemented without delay and made available to the competent authorities for inspections. Beside the obligatory systems, there are facultative quality management systems. In respective to food packaging operators there are functioning:

- ISO 9001:2008 Quality management systems – Requirements.
- ISO 22000:2005 Food safety management systems – Requirements for organizations throughout the food chain.
- EN 15593:2008 Packaging– Management of hygiene in the manufacture of packaging for food requirements.
- The BRC/IOP Global Standard for Packaging & Packaging Materials.

ISO 9001:2008 outlines the specifications for a quality management system and aims to improve customer satisfaction through the efficient use of the system. The organization must be able to show that it can consistently deliver a product that satisfies customer needs as well as applicable legal and regulatory requirements. Moreover, including processes for continual improvement of the system and the assurance of conformity to customer and applicable statutory and regulatory requirements (ISO 9001:2008).

ISO 22000:2005 outlines the specifications for a food safety management system, whereby a chain of food companies must prove that it can control dangers related to food safety, including those arising from food packaging, in order to guarantee food safety when consumed by humans. It is relevant to all businesses, regardless of size. The system is intended for operators that wish to put in place systems that reliably deliver safe products and are involved in any part of the food chain, such as production, distribution, packaging, and packing. (ISO 22000:2005).

The EN 15593 Standard is devoted to all organizations that want to effectively manage the hygiene in the production of packaging for food. The requirements of the standard include health management system, hazard analysis and risk assessment, pollution sources and requirements for plants and personnel. EN 15593 can be a tool to improve the quality management system for packaging of food (EN 15593:2009).

The BRC/IOP Global Standard for Packaging & Packaging Materials is dedicated to packaging sector companies which produce packaging and packaging materials used in the food and non-food industry. The main idea in creating the standard was to provide an efficient tool for the packaging industry to ensure consumers safety and fulfillment of legal requirements (BRC/IOP Global Standard for Packaging & Packaging Materials).

Packaging is a very important element in product quality maintenance that is why quality of packaging has great influence and its quality assurance is necessary. Physical flow in the supply chain may deteriorate some packaging features, so their monitoring and proper conditions of storage, transport and suitable protection are important. Following the procedure of quality management systems is the guarantee of packaging quality assurance. The requirements of implemented systems are different in each packaging risk category. Although functioning obligatory and facultative quality management systems it is essential their conscious implementation and monitoring of their activity for proper adjustment to packaging risk category. Only those activities might bring expected and effective results.

It is necessary to conduct continuous monitoring of obligatory quality assurance systems implementation in enterprises constituting packaging supply chains. It is important for consumer protection policy fulfillment, which is one of the basis of common market rule in the European Union.

GMPs

The safety of food packaging is as important as that of the food itself. A Good Manufacturing Practice (GMP) program addresses the safety of food contact materials and products by: implementing reasonable control processes and establishing appropriate quality systems. GMP programs ensure food contact materials and products comply with applicable regulations and are of suitable purity for intended uses. GMPs are required by various regulations throughout the world, such as US FDA 21CFR174.5, and EU Commission Regulation (EC) No 2023/2006. A GMP program can be used to collect data and information necessary to demonstrate compliance to these regulations.

The purpose of GMP is to prevent contamination in manufacturing, storage and transportation and to ensure food contact materials and products are safe for their intended uses. In addition, a well-established quality system in a GMP program will address any material or product safety or contamination-related incident with the most effective corrective action plan.

The best GMP program addresses the whole production cycle of food contact material and products. It starts with selection of the materials, the incoming raw material quality control and proper storage, production equipment cleaning procedures, manufacturing facility housekeeping procedures, material traceability and product QA and QC control, management of change, employee training and facility auditing, product packaging, storage and shipping, and so on.

A well designed GMP program takes into consideration the type of product that is produced and the position of the product in the overall manufacturing process and supply chain. For example, a GMP program for the manufacture of an additive chemical used in plastics to achieve certain technical function, will be different from a GMP program for a manufacturing facility that makes containers to pack cooked food in for long-term storage before consumer use.

As GMP is a regulatory requirement for manufacturing food contact materials and products, it is to the benefit of the manufacturer to design and implement a quality GMP program that is relevant to the product.

HACCP

HACCP (Hazard Analysis and Critical Control Points) is "a systematic approach to the identification, evaluation, and control of food safety hazards." It is an internationally recognized system used to identify and control Food Safety hazards. It is a preventative approach to Food Safety developed in the early 1970s by the Pillsbury Company and NASA, the National Aeronautics and Space Administration.

The Packaging HACCP Models are intended to be used by companies supplying packaging components to food producers. They may be used by those packaging companies that are just beginning to implement HACCP and those wishing to evaluate their existing plan.

Food manufacturers' suppliers of packaging are included in the food business. Food safety is ensured from the point of consumption to the packaging provider. Packaging suppliers are crucial allies for food safety, particularly those who work directly with products or with printed materials.

A set of guidelines called the Packaging HACCP Models is intended to help food packaging manufacturers set up and carry out a HACCP program. Their purpose is to offer direction when creating HACCP plans. The Food Safety Alliance for Packaging (FSAP) is the organization that developed the Packaging HACCP Models. Initiative of the Food Safety Alliance for Packaging (FSAP): Major food corporations, packaging companies, food industry associations, and consultants are involved in the FSAP Initiative project. The team's main objective is to advise packaging firms, with a focus on issues pertaining to food safety and packaging. The FSAP works to increase public awareness of food packaging safety and to give the packaging supply chain access to resources and training.

Procedure

Common Approach for HACCP Implementation -

a) Assemble HACCP Team (multi-disciplinary).

b) Write Product Description (how is it made and what raw materials are used)

c) Identify Target Audience (include markets and customers)

d) Create Process Flow Diagram

e) Verify Process Flow Diagram

f) Identify Hazards

g) Perform Hazard Analysis

h) Determine if Critical Control Points (CCP) exist (Some processes will not have CCPs)

k) Establish Corrective Actions for Critical Control Point Deviations (if applicable)

l) Verify HACCP Plan

i) Establish Critical Control Point Limits (if applicable)

j) Establish Monitoring Procedures for Critical Control Points (if applicable)

HACCP Validation

Validation and Verification of HACCP Plans In summary, Validation verifies that the HACCP plan appropriately addresses the relevant activities, and Verification verifies that the HACCP plan is being followed. Documentation of validation and verification procedures is required.

Verification involves a variety of tasks, including reviewing HACCP records, conducting prior HACCP plan audits, spot-checking prerequisite programs, and conducting an annual internal (or external) audit to ensure the HACCP plan is being followed exactly. It also involves verifying operator training and competence in monitoring CCPs and addressing out-of-compliances. Verification ensures that the HACCP plan is consistently and successfully implemented.

Validation entails tasks including evaluating the hazard analysis critically for correctness and depth (i.e., were all dangers taken into account? Are the critical limits relevant and actionable? Were the correct CCPs selected? Critical review of the CCPs; and monitoring activities (i.e., are the right metrics monitored at the right frequency?). Validation offers proof that the strategies and tactics used by the plant are practical and effective for that particular plant, not simply in principle.

Inference

Experiment 17

Examination of Canned Food by Cut Out Method

Objective

After performing this experiment you will be able to:

Perform the cut out test for the given sample of food product.

Principle

The cut-out test is conducted to evaluate the overall quality of canned food. This test involves examining the condition of the food contents, the external and internal state of the can, and other characteristics of the product through various organoleptic, physical, and chemical assessments.

Materials and Equipment

1. Canned food: 4-6 nos. Cans
2. Tone tester
3. Physical balance
4. Vacuum gauge
5. Can opener
6. Brix refractometer
7. Scale
8. pH paper near neutral ranges.

Procedure

1. Label Details: If the cans are labeled, note the details of the label.
2. Embossed Code: Record the embossed code mark on the lid.
3. External Condition: Observe the external condition of the cans for rusting, dents, physical damage, seam defects, etc.
4. Fill and Vacuum Test: Test the tone of the can to assess the fill level and vacuum.
5. Gross Weight: Determine the gross weight of the can.
6. Vacuum Measurement: Measure the vacuum inside the can.

7. Lid Removal and Observation: Cut the lid almost completely open and observe the surface of the food and the inside of the lid. Measure the headspace.
8. Drain Contents: Drain the contents for 5 minutes and collect the liquid in a measuring jar.
9. Liquid Analysis: Note the volume, turbidity, color, texture, flavor, etc., and check for any foreign matter.
10. Can Interior: Observe the bottom and inside of the can for settled curds.
11. Empty Can Weight: Wash, dry, and weigh the empty can.

Observation

Name of Product	
Brand Name	
Net Weight	
Drained Weight	
Best Before Date	
FSSAI License Number	
Batch Number	
Date of Manufacture	
Manufactured and Packed by	
Diameter of Can	
Diameter of Lid	
Length of Can	
Seam Thickness	
Seam Length	
Weight of Can + Sample	
Temperature	
pH of Brine	
pH of Product	
Volume of Brine	
Drained Weight	
Specific Gravity	
Total Seam Thickness	
TSS (Total Soluble Solids) of Sugar Syrup	
TSS of Solid	
Thickness of Lid	
Thickness of Can	
Titre Value of Product	
Titre Value of Brine	
% Acidity of Product	

Product name	
Brand name	
Lot no.	
Mfd. Date	
MRP	
Best before	
Net weight	
Gross weight	
Temperature	
Seam thickness	
Seam length	
Dimensions	
Container-product	

Inference

Experiment 18

To Study the Effect of Can Close Temperature on the Resultant Vacuum Produced

---

Objective

After performing this experiment you will be able to learn:

The effect of can close temperature on the resultant vacuum produced.

Principle

The unfilled volume of the hermetic (air-tight) food container usually referred to as the ***headspace***, is a most important part of the container –contents system. In the majority of canned foods, the headspace consists of air and water vapor. Whereas a canned food would keep for a long time i.e. minimum two years of shelf life, stable, only if a certain degree of vacuum is created inside the can. The degree to which air has been extracted from a hermetic food container is measured by the pressure inside, which is referred to as vacuum. A vacuum of -101 kPa would mean that all of the gas has been expelled from the container; a vacuum of zero would mean that the pressure in the headspace is equal to atmospheric pressure. The difference between the pressure within the container and the air pressure is measured by a vacuum gauge.

Since the absence of oxygen will prevent

a) Microorganism to grow and thereby will not bring about changes in flavor and taste.

b) It prevents oxidation of fat

c) It prevent destruction of vitamin C

d) It also prevents internal corrosion of the can during storage period.

Proper exhausting of canned foods before retorting is an important operation.

Vacuum in cans may be created by:

- **Heat exhausting or hot filling**- the contents of the can are heated to a temperature of 80-90°C prior to seaming to expand the product, expand and drive out occluded and dissolved gasses in the product,and reduce the air in the headspace. Contraction of the contents of the can after seaming and cooling produces a vacuum. If the filling temperature is too high (96ºC) 'paneling' of the cans may occur (i.e. the walls of the can will collapse in on cooling).

- **Mechanical methods** using vacuum Seamer.
- **Steam injection method**: Steam is injected into the headspace in such a way so as to sweep out air, replacing it with steam. The can is then immediately sealed. The vacuum is produced when steam in the can condenses.

In exhausting by heat, the most significant factor is the study of how the vacuum produced in can varies with the final temperature attained before closing.

Procedure

Materials & Equipment

1. Empty cans, about 30 Nos. (No.1 Tall).
2. Water for filling to heat at different temperatures.
3. Physical balance for weighing.
4. Double Seaming machine
5. Scale, vacuum gauge,
6. Thermometers etc.

Procedures

1. Divide the cans into 6 groups of 5 cans each.
2. Note the weight of each empty can.
3. Fill each group with water at different temperatures (40ºC, 50ºC. 60ºC) up to a head–space of 10 mm.
4. Weigh each can.
5. Note the temperature of water in each can and immediately double seam.
6. Cool all the cans to room temperature (To be noted). Wipe and dry the outside of the cans and reweigh to check spillage if any.
7. Test vacuum produced in each can and Find out-group averages.
8. Open the cans and note the temperature of vacuum measurement. Measure headspace also.
9. Tabulate and plot can vacuum against closing temperature.

Observation

Group	Can No.	Gross Wt. (gm)	Closing Temp. (°C)	Can vacuum at		Head space (mm)	Remarks
				Cms	°C		
A	1.					10	
	2.					10	
	3.					10	
	4.					10	
	5.					10	
	Average		40			10	
B	1.					10	
	2.					10	
	3.					10	
	4.					10	
	5.					10	
	Average		50			10	
C	1.					10	
	2.					10	
	3.					10	
	4.					10	
	5.					10	
	Average		60			10	

Inference

Experiment 19

To Determine Thermal Shock Resistance in Glass

Objective

After performing this experiment you will be able to learn:

Thermal Shock Resistance in Glass.

Principle

Thermal shock occurs when different parts of an object expand at different rates due to a thermal gradient. This differential expansion creates stress or strain within the material. If this stress exceeds the material's strength, it can lead to the formation of cracks. If these cracks are not stopped from propagating, they can cause the material to fail structurally. Thermal shock is quantified by the temperature difference between the heated temperature T1 and the cold water bath temperature T2 to which the object is subsequently exposed, which can reveal any cracks or damage.

Purpose of Thermal Shock Test

Glass items often experience significant temperature changes during normal use, and the thermal shock test is designed to ensure their resistance to such conditions. For example, moving a casserole dish from a hot oven to a cool countertop might be enough to cause it to break. This test evaluates the quality, durability, and strength of glass packaging materials used for both solid and liquid food products.

Stages of Thermal Shock Resistance Test

1. **Pass Test**: A sample is considered to have passed if no more than an agreed number of items are cracked or broken after being subjected to a specified thermal shock (T1−T2).
2. **Progressive Test to a Specified Percentage of Breakages**: Containers that pass the initial test are subjected to progressively higher temperature gradients (T1−T2) until a predetermined percentage of containers fail.

3. **Total Progressive Test**: All containers are tested with increasing temperature gradients until every container fails.

Products That Can Be Tested

Thermal shock testing is applicable to a variety of glass products, including:

- Bottles and jars
- Cookware and kitchenware
- Toiletry and cosmetic containers
- Domestic wares such as bowls, vases, drinking vessels, latte cups, and mugs
- Candle holders, candle jars, and hurricane lamps
- Technical, industrial, and pharmaceutical glassware

Procedure

1. **Prepare the Water Baths**:
    - Fill both the hot and cold water baths with water.
    - Record the temperature of the cold water bath.
    - Adjust the temperature of the hot water bath so that the difference between the hot and cold water bath temperatures is 43°C.
2. **Heating**:
    - Allow the hot water bath to reach the desired temperature.
    - Place a wire basket with the bottles into the hot water bath, allowing the bottles to fill with water.
    - Leave the bottles in the hot water bath for 15 minutes.
3. **Cooling**:
    - Quickly transfer the wire basket with the bottles to the cold water bath within 10 seconds.
    - Fully immerse the bottles in the cold water bath, ensuring no cold water enters the bottles.
    - Keep the bottles in the cold water bath for 2 minutes.
4. **Inspection**:
    - Remove the bottles from the cold water bath and check for any visible cracks or damage.
5. **Repeat**:
    - Repeat steps 2 to 4, increasing the temperature gradient by 10°C each time, until cracks appear.

Observation

A total of ………… sample bottles were taken for thermal shock testing.

Observation Table (Glass Sample)

Time (Mins)	Temperature - T_1 (°C)	Temperature - T_2 (°C)	Temperature Gradient (T_1-T_2) (°C)	Breakages

Example

Fresh Sample Bottle before Thermal Shock Test

Cracks seen in 2 bottles after the 2nd Thermal Shock (i.e, after 30mins with a temperature gradient of 73°C)

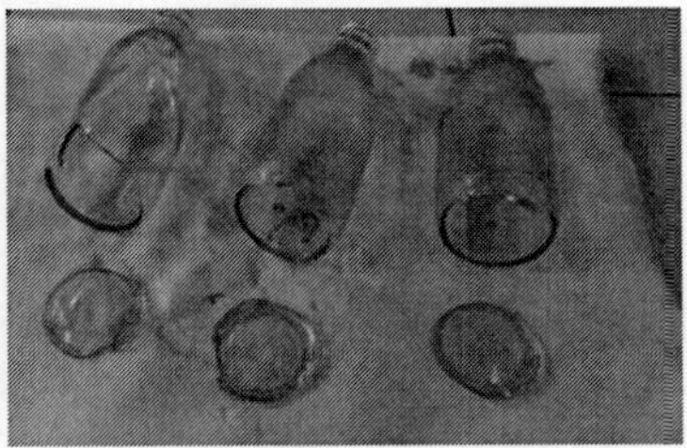

Cracks seen after 3rd Thermal Shock (i.e, after 45mins with a temperature gradient of 80°C)

Inference

Experiment 20

Determination of Porosity of Tin Plate

Objective

After performing this experiment you will be able to learn

Determination of porosity of tin plate.

Introduction

Porosity in tinplate refers to the presence of tiny holes or pores in the tin coating on steel sheets used for making tin cans. These pores can expose the underlying steel to the contents of the can, potentially leading to corrosion and contamination of the food product. Ensuring minimal porosity is crucial for maintaining the integrity and safety of food packaging. Tinplate is produced by coating a thin layer of tin onto a steel sheet. This can be done through hot-dipping or electroplating. The goal is to create a uniform and continuous tin layer that acts as a protective barrier against corrosion. During the coating process, imperfections such as pores or pinholes can form in the tin layer. These imperfections can occur due to variations in the coating thickness, impurities in the tin, or mechanical damage during handling and processing.When a tinplate can with porosity is filled with food, the contents can come into direct contact with the exposed steel through the pores.The acidic or basic nature of certain food products can accelerate the corrosion of the exposed steel, leading to the formation of rust.This corrosion can compromise the structural integrity of the can and potentially contaminate the food with rust particles or harmful by-products of the corrosion process. The primary function of the tin coating is to act as a physical barrier that prevents the food from contacting the steel. A continuous and defect-free tin layer ensures effective protection.Tin also provides cathodic protection to the steel. In the presence of an electrolyte (e.g., acidic food), tin acts as the sacrificial anode, corroding preferentially to the steel. However, this mechanism is only effective if the tin layer is relatively thick and the porosity is minimal.

Testing for Porosity

The Ferricyanide paper test is a simple and effective method used to detect porosity in tinplate. This test helps identify the presence of pores or pinholes in the tin coating that could expose the underlying steel to corrosion, especially important in food packaging.

Principle

The Ferricyanide paper test is based on the reaction between exposed iron (from the steel substrate) and a ferricyanide solution. When ferricyanide ions come into contact with iron, they form a blue-colored complex known as Prussian blue. This color change indicates the presence of pores in the tin coating where the steel is exposed.

Ferricyanide solution preparation: Add 1 gm of Potassium ferricyanide and 0.5 gram sodium chloride in 100 ml of distilled water.

Procedure for Ferricyanide Paper Test on Tinplate

Cut tinplate samples to 8 cm × 5.5 cm.

Clean and degrease the samples using carbon tetrachloride (CCl_4), then dry.

Cut a filter paper strip to the same size as the tinplate sample.

Moisten the filter paper with a ferricyanide solution containing 0.5 grams of Tergitol 08.

Place the moistened filter paper on the tinplate sample, ensuring good contact.

Keep the paper in contact for one hour, re-moistening as needed without over-wetting to prevent spot diffusion

Remove the test paper and dry.

Count the blue spots on the paper and record as a measure of porosity, expressed as the number of blue spots per square decimeter (100 square centimeters) of the tinplate.

This procedure is suitable for hot-dipped tinplate but not for electrolytic tinplate, which gives a uniform color with the test paper.

Inference

Experiment 21

Identification of Paper and Paperboard

Objective

After performing this experiment you will be able to learn:

Identification of paper and paperboard.

Introduction

Paper can be broadly classified into two categories: coarse papers, which are normally made of unbleached Kraft softwood pulp and used for packing, and fine papers, which are usually composed of bleached pulp and used for writing paper, bond, ledger, book, and cover sheets.

The main types of packaging papers are:

Kraft paper

Usually produced on a Fourdrinier machine, kraft paper is gritty and incredibly strong. It is then either machine-glazed on a Yankee dryer or machine-finished on a calendar. Sometimes it isn't calendared so that the rough surface will keep the bags from slipping over one another when they're stacked on pallets.

Bleached paper

Relatively white, brilliant, and soft pulps are used to make bleached paper. Compared to unbleached paper, it is weaker and more expensive. One or both of its sides may be coated with clay to increase its visual appeal.

Greaseproof paper

Translucent machine-finished paper that has been hydrated to provide oil and grease resistance is known as greaseproof paper. The cellulose fibers are broken and fibrillated by prolonged beating or mechanical refinement, which causes the fibers to absorb so much water that they appear sticky and superficially gelatinized. Hydration is a physical phenomena that causes the paper machine's web to consolidate and fill up a large number of the interstitial spaces.

The degree to which the pores have been sealed determines how well greaseproof papers work. Since they prevent fat from penetrating for a respectable amount of time, they are frequently used to package butter and other comparable fatty goods.

Glassine paper

The name "glassine" refers to the smooth, glassy surface, high density, and transparency of this material. Greaseproof paper is further processed in a supercalender, which involves delicately dampening it with water and passing it through a series of rollers heated by steam. As a result, there are so few holes or other fiber/air interfaces for light scattering or liquid penetration that the refractive index of the glassine paper approaches the 0 value of amorphous cellulose. This indicates that the interfiber hydrogen bonding is so intimate. The degree to which the pulp is hydrated can have a significant impact on the transparency. The titanium dioxide adds an opaque quality, and the paper is often plasticized to make it more durable.

Vegetable parchment

In order to make parchment paper, a web of superior, unsized chemical pulp is immersed in a bath of pure sulfuric acid. Extensive hydrogen bonding is produced as the cellulose fibers expand and partially disintegrate, filling the spaces between the fibers. It is resistant to grease and oils, free of lint, odor, and taste, and stronger when wet than when dry.

Due to its resilience to grease and its moist strength, it may be easily removed from food materials without defibrillating, making it useful as a food interleaver between pieces of meat or pastry. Often used in items with a high oil or grease content, parchment is used to make labels and inserts. Cheese and other foodstuffs are wrapped with it.

Waxed paper

Papers that have been waxed offer protection from liquid and vapor penetration. The three main varieties are wax laminated, dry waxed, and wet waxed.

Wet-waxed papers are produced by shock-chilling the waxed web right away after the wax is applied, resulting in a continuous surface film on one or both sides. Additionally, this gives the coated surface a high sheen. Dry-waxed papers don't have a continuous layer on their surfaces because they are made with heated rollers. As a result, the exposed strands draw moisture into the paper and function as wicks.

Paperboard Products

Paper is generally termed board when its grammage exceeds 224g m^2. Multiply boards are produced by the consolidation of one or more wen plies into a single sheet of paperboard, which is then subsequently used to manufacture rigid boxes, folding cartons, beverage cartons and similar products. One advantage of multi-ply forming is the ability to utilize inexpensive and bulky low-grade waste materials (mostly old newspapers and other post consumer waste papers) in the inner piles of board where low fiber strength and the presence of extraneous materials (e.g. inks, coatings etc.) have little effect on board properties. However, multi-ply boards containing post consumer waste papers are not used for food contact purposes.

Paperboard Grades

Linerboard: board having at least two piles, the top layer being of relatively better quality; usually made on a Fourdrinier with 100% virgin pulp furnish.

Foodboard: Board used for food packaging having a single or multi-ply construction usually made from 100% bleached virgin pulp furnish.

Folding Boxboard (Cartonboard): Multi-ply board used to make folding boxes, top ply (liner 0 is made from virgin pulp and the other plies are made from secondary fiber.

Chipboard: Multiply board made from 100% low grade secondary fiber.

Base board: Board that will ultimately be coated or covered.

Folding Cartons

Folding cartons are containers made from sheets of paper board (typically with thickness between 300 and 1100 um) which have been cut and scored for bending into desired shape.

Kinds of Folding Cartons Boxes: the carton boxes are grouped into 6

1. Group A- Long seam glued folding cartons with rectangular surfaces
2. Group B- Folding cartons with rectangular surfaces and non long seam glued
3. Group C- Long seam glued folding cartons with non- rectangular surfaces
4. Group D- Folding cartons with non rectangular surfaces non long seam glued
5. Group E- Product integrated folding carton
6. Group F- Other folding carton

Beverage Cartons

The carton normally consists of layers of bleached and unbleached paperboard coated internally and externally with LDPE resulting in a carton that is impermeable to liquids and in which the internal and external surfaces may be heat sealed. There may also be a thin layer aluminum foil which acts as a gas and light barrier. Incorporation of an aluminum foil layer allows a longer shelf life for premium juice products.

Differentiation of cardboard on the basis of flute

Flute Designation	Flute Per Linear Foot	Flutes Thickness (in.)
A Flute	33+3	3/16
B Flute	47+3	1/8
C Flute	39+3	5/32
D Flute	90+4	1/16

Corrugated board consists of one or two outer plies, the flutes and, in multi-ply types of corrugated board, of one or more intermediate plies. Corrugated board is classified as follows according to the number of outer/intermediate plies and flutes:

Single face corrugated board

Single face corrugated board consists of one ply of fluted paper, onto which paper or cardboard is glued.

Single wall corrugated board

Single wall (double face) corrugated board consists of one ply of fluted paper which is glued between two piles of paper or cardboard.

Double wall corrugated board

Double wall corrugated board consists of two plies of fluted paper which are glued together by one ply of unfluted paper or cardboard and the exposed outer surfaces of which are each covered with one ply of paper or cardboard.

Tri-wall corrugated board

Tri-wall corrugated board consists of three plies of fluted paper which are glued together by two plies of paper or cardboard and the outer surfaces of which are likewise each covered with one ply of paper or cardboard.

Procedure

1. Observe the edges of each sample.
2. Then with the help of Vernier calipers measure the thickness of the sample and identify the type of corrugated board.
3. Note your observations.

Observation

Sample No.	Flutes Thickness (in.)	Type of Corrugated Board

Inference

Experiment 22

Edible Packaging of Food Sample

Objective

After performing this experiment you will be able to learn:

How to do edible packaging of food sample.

Introduction

Edible Packaging – An edible film or coating is simply defined as a thin continuous layer of edible material formed on, placed on, or between the foods or food components. The package is an integral part of the food, which can be eaten as a part of the whole food product.

Edible packaging can be done in two types:

Edible coating: Edible coating are applied and formed directly on food (e.g. by spraying, immersion, and fluidization) via a coating solution. This will be a part of the food and must not provoke unwanted change (organoleptic, physical, and chemical).

Edible films: Edible films are produced by (casting, extrusion, compression, and molding) and only then applied on foods.

The edible films are environment friendly, can be fully consumed or is biodegradable. It can reduce the waste and solid disposal problem and enhance organoleptic properties like color, sweetness etc. And this can be used as micro encapsulation of flavoring agents.

Edible film can also be characterized on two bases

1. **Starch based:** Edible films made from starch are tasteless, odorless and transparent thus preventing a change in taste flavor and appearance of food products.

   Advantage: Starch films are excellent barrier properties to O_2 and CO_2 on the other hand it has weaker barrier properties to the water/moisture due to hydrophilicity.

2 **Protein based**: Protein based films exhibit poor water resistance and lower mechanical strength. It has greater mechanical & barrier properties which are generally superior to polysaccharides. Proteins are good film former exhibiting excellent gas and lipid barrier properties.

Advantage: Protein films are brittle and susceptible to crackling due to the strong cohesive energy density of the polymer.

Procedure

- Take 9.5 gm corn starch in a beaker, add 60 ml of water in it and mix it properly through a magnetic stirrer.
- Then add 5 ml of glycerin in it with continuous mixing.
- Then add 5-7% acetic acid (vinegar) and again mix the whole solution properly.
- After complete mixing turn on the heat and heat the mixture till it become viscous.
- Then evenly spread the viscous fluid on aluminum foil using a spoon or a bowl surface and spread it as thin as possible.
- Cool it for some time and dry it for 7 days.
- After drying, measure its thickness by vernier calipers.
- Calculate its heat sealing capacity by heat sealer and see the printability with the help of stamp or marker.

Observation

S.No.	Properties	Observation
1	Thickness	
2	Printability	
3	Heat Sealing Strength	
4	Transprancy	

Inference

Experiment 23

To Study Physical Tests of Given Sample

Objective

After performing this experiment you will be able to learn:

Physical tests of packaging material.

I. Determination of Machine Direction

Introduction

Machine-made paper has two directions and two sides:

Directions

a) Machine Direction: The direction in which the paper or board aligns with the flow of material on the paper machine.

b) Cross Direction: The direction perpendicular to the machine direction

Procedure

- Cut a small rectangular or circular piece from the sample paper and place it into a beaker containing water.
- After some time, the test piece will start to curl.
- Observe the direction of the curl.
- The axis along which the paper curls indicates the machine direction of the paper.

Inference

II. Determination of Top Side and Wire Side

Introduction

a) Wire Side: The side of the paper that was in contact with the wire of the paper machine during its production.

b) Top Side: The side of the paper opposite to the wire side.

Procedure

- Follow the same procedure as outlined for the determination of the machine direction.
- When the test piece curls, the convex side of the curl will indicate the wire side of the paper.
- The opposite side will be the top side of the paper.

Inference

III. Determination of Basic Weight or Grammage

Introduction

The basis weight, or grammage, represents the weight per unit area of paper. While not a fundamental property, it is significant when reporting other physical properties, such as bursting strength, and also impacts the cost factor.

Procedure

- Cut a test sample in the form of a rectangle of any convenient size.
- Measure each side to calculate the area.
- Weigh the test specimen.

Calculations

Use the formula to calculate the grammage (G):

$$G = \frac{W}{A} \times 10,000$$

Where:

- G is the grammage in grams per square meter (gsm.)
- W is the Weight of the Paper sample in grams.
- A is the area of the Paper sample in square centimeters

Inference

Experiment 24

To Study Moisture Content of Given Sample

Objective

After performing this experiment you will be able to learn:

Moisture content of packaging material.

Introduction

The moisture content of paper is a critical parameter that significantly affects its other properties, such as printing quality and absorbency. Maintaining an optimal moisture level is essential for ensuring the functionality and durability of the paper. For instance, double-faced corrugated boards tend to break or crack during bending operations if they are too dry.

Procedure

- Weigh the conditioned specimen and place it in a drying oven, maintained at a temperature of 103°C ± 2°C, to expel moisture. Continue heating until a constant weight is achieved.
- If the moisture content of the paper is to be determined "as received," the sample should not be conditioned.
- Weigh the unconditioned sample and place it in the drying oven, maintaining the temperature at 103°C ± 2°C for approximately 2 hours.
- Re-weigh the sample. Repeat the process of drying and weighing periodically until the difference in weight between two successive measurements is no more than 0.1% of the specimen's weight.

Calculations

$$\text{Moisture Content (\%)} = \frac{\text{Wet Weight} - \text{Dry Weight}}{\text{Wet Weight}} \times 100^{1}$$

Inference

Experiment 25

To Study Mildew (Fungus) Resistance of Paper and Paper Board Sample

Objective

After performing this experiment you will be able to learn:

Mildew resistance packaging material.

Introduction

Studying the mildew resistance of paper involves evaluating how well the paper can resist fungal growth under specific conditions. Mildew, a type of mold, can degrade paper quality, causing discoloration, weakening, and unpleasant odors. Here's a detailed procedure to assess the mildew resistance of paper:

Materials Needed

Paper samples (different types, if comparison is required), Sterile petri dishes, Sterile distilled water

Fungal spore suspension (commonly Aspergillus niger or similar mildew spores), Nutrient medium (e.g., potato dextrose agar or a similar agar that promotes fungal growth), Incubator, Sterile tweezers and scissors, Forceps, Micropipette or dropper, Humidity chamber (can be a sealed container with a saturated salt solution to maintain high humidity), Control samples (untreated paper).

Procedure

- Preparation of Paper Samples:
- Cut the paper samples into uniform pieces (e.g., 5 cm × 5 cm).
- Sterilize the samples by autoclaving or using another suitable method to ensure no initial fungal contamination.
- Preparation of Nutrient Medium:
- Prepare the nutrient medium according to the manufacturer's instructions and pour it into sterile petri dishes.
- Allow the medium to solidify.

- Inoculation with Fungal Spores:
- Prepare a spore suspension by mixing fungal spores in sterile distilled water.
- Using a micropipette or dropper, apply a small amount of the spore suspension onto the surface of each paper sample.
- Spread the suspension evenly over the paper surface using a sterile loop or spreader.
- Placement on Nutrient Medium:
- Place the inoculated paper samples on the surface of the solidified nutrient medium in the petri dishes.
- Ensure the samples have good contact with the agar.

Incubation

- Place the petri dishes in an incubator set to a temperature conducive to fungal growth, typically around 25-28°C.

Maintain a high humidity environment by placing the petri dishes in a humidity chamber or sealed container with a saturated salt solution.

Observation Period

- Incubate the samples for a specified period, usually 7-14 days.
- Regularly check the samples for signs of mildew growth, noting any visible fungal colonies on the paper.

Evaluation

After the incubation period, assess the extent of mildew growth on the paper samples.

Use a rating scale to quantify the level of mildew resistance. For example:

0: No visible growth
1: Very slight growth
2: Slight growth
3: Moderate growth
4: Heavy growth

Compare the results to control samples (untreated paper) to determine the relative mildew resistance of each paper type.

Documentation

Document the findings with photographs and detailed notes on the extent of mildew growth.

Calculate the percentage of the paper surface area affected by mildew.

Reporting Results

Present the results in a tabulated form showing the level of mildew growth for each paper sample.

Include photographs for visual reference.

Discuss the implications of the results for the suitability of each paper type in environments prone to high humidity and mildew exposure.

Precautions

Ensure all procedures are conducted under sterile conditions to prevent contamination.

Consider repeating the experiment with multiple replicates to ensure reliability and reproducibility of the results.

Evaluate the potential need for antifungal treatments or coatings on paper intended for use in high-humidity environments.

Inference

Experiment 26

To Study pH of Given Sample

Objective

After performing this experiment you will be able to learn:

pH value of packaging material.

Introduction

As mentioned earlier, these tests are performed to assess the suitability of the board for printing, corrosion protection, food packaging etc. The presence of acid in paper or paper possessing an acidic reaction is a property of specific importance. Not only may the presence of acid effect the aging properties of paper, but it also may act upon materials that come into contact with the paper. In addition, the sizing of paper, wet strength treatment, and dye and fillers retention, usually depend upon the addition of alum or other acidic materials to the beater furnish. Hence many appers are acidic to various degrees at the time of manufacture. pH is a measure of hydrogen ion present which depends both upon the amount of acidic material and upon its degree of ionization. Hence, pH does not measure the amount of acid present. Since it is the 'activity or 'intensity' of acid that is usually of most interest, the pH value is the more common test.

Procedure

1. A known weight of the test specimen is extracted with distilled water.
2. pH of supernatant liquid is found out and compared with the blank reading.
3. The accurate determination of pH value becomes important in the case of papers intended for use in permanent records. In such cases a pH value of not less than 5.0 is required.
4. It is also possible to determine the quantity of acid in paper, by titrating an extract of the paper with standard alkali solution using phenolphthalein indicator.

Calculations

Percentage of acidity in terms SO_3 = (T-t)* N* 0.04* 100 / W

Where,

T = NaOH required for titration of extract

t = titration of the blank

N = Normality of NaOH

W = Weight of specimen in gram

Inference

Experiment 27

To Study
Grease Resistance of Given Sample

Objective

After performing this experiment you will be able to learn :

Grease resistance of packaging material.

Equipment

Test tube of any rigid material of 1 in. inside diameter and 1 in. in length, pipette, sand, Brook paper and stopwatch.

Introduction

Grease resistance testing is used to measure the repellence of paper and board materials to grease, oil and waxes.Certain varieties of products require grease resistant papers. e.g. in the packaging of butter, cheese, etc. Grease resistance of paper is determined by the time taken by turpentine to penetrate through the paper. This test is usually applied to greaseproof, glassine, vegetable parchment. It is not always suitable for assessing papers and boards that are given grease or oil resistance by means of a coating or internal treatment.

Procedure

- The apparatus essentially consists of a tube of any rigid material of 1 in. inside diameter and 1 in. in length.
- The test specimen is placed on a plain paper. Place the end of the tube on the specimen and put 5 gm of sand in the tube. Since the purpose of the tube is to assure a uniform area of the sand pile, remove it immediately after the addition of the sand.
- Using the dropper, add 1.1 ml of the coloured turpentine to the sand and note the time.
- Move the test specimen to different positions on the plain paper and examine the uncovered area of it for staining after every 30 sec.

1. Procedure is continued till staining appears on the plain paper.

2. The time interval of addition of turpentine and observance of the red stain in seconds is recorded as the transudation time or in other words this is called the turpentine test.

Inference

S.No.	Paper Sample	Felt Side	Wire Side	Time in Seconds